EDWARD ALBEE

EDWARD ALBEE
An Interview and Essays

Edited by
JULIAN N. WASSERMAN
Associate Editors
JOY L. LINSLEY & JEROME A. KRAMER

Lee Lecture Series
The University of St. Thomas   Houston, Texas
1983

Quotations and passages from the following plays of Edward Albee are reprinted with the permission of Coward, McCann & Geoghegan, Inc.: *The American Dream*, copyright© 1960, 1961 Edward Albee; *The Zoo Story*, copyright © 1960 Edward Albee.

Quotations and passages from the following plays of Edward Albee are reprinted with the permission of Atheneum publishers: *Who's Afraid of Virginia Woolf?*, copyright© 1962 Edward Albee; *Tiny Alice*, copyright © 1965 Edward Albee; *A Delicate Balance*, copyright © 1969 Edward Albee; *All Over*, copyright © 1971 Edward Albee; *Seascape*, copyright© 1975 Edward Albee; *Counting the Ways*, copyright © 1975 Edward Albee; *Listening*, copyright © 1976 Edward Albee; *The Lady from Dubuque*, copyright © 1980 Edward Albee.

Library of Congress Cataloging in Publication Data
Main entry under title:

Edward Albee: an interview and essays.

(Lee lectures series)
Includes index.
1. Albee, Edward, 1928– –Criticism and interpretation. 2. Albee, Edward, 1928– –Interviews. I. Albee, Edward, 1928– . II. Wasserman, Julian N. III. Linsley, Joy L. IV. Kramer, Jerome A., 1936– .
V. Series.
PS3511.L25Z66 1983   812'.54   82-20006
ISBN 0-8156-8106-2
ISBNo-8156-8107-0 (pbk.)

Manufactured in the United States of America

In Memory of
FATHER EDWARD GREGORY LEE, C.S.B.
1901–1976

Acknowledgments

In 1977, friends, colleagues, and students of the late Fr. Edward Lee established the Lee Lectureship in order to bring prominent figures from the Arts and Humanities to the University of St. Thomas campus. Without the help and support of Fr. P. Wallace Platt and Dr. Joy Linsley, neither Mr. Albee's appearance at the University nor this volume would have been possible. The editors would also like to thank the following people for their generous support of the Lee Lectureship:

Mr. Al Albrecht
Miss Blake Anderson
Mr. Leland W. Anderson
Mr. George T. Barrow
Mr. John Bradshaw
Brazos Bookstore
Mr. Ted Brown
Mr. Tex Bruno
Dr. and Mrs. John W. Clark
Mr. Franklin Cover
Mr. Richard M. Cranston
Mr. Andre Crispin
Mr. John Crispin
Mr. and Mrs. Robert W. Davis Jr.
Mrs. Ed Dawley
Mrs. John De Menil
Mr. and Mrs. Charles Fischer
Ms. E. A. Harth
Mr. and Mrs. John Heyburn
Dr. Gwendlyn A. Howell
Mr. and Mrs. Albert Kaeppel
Mrs. Edith Lee

Mr. Lawrence J. Madigan
Ms. Catherine Mallon
Sr. Joan Markey, S.S.M.
Dr. Peggy McCormack
Mr. Frank Melady
Metallurgical Consultants, Inc.
Mr. and Mrs. Charles Molesworth
Mrs. Richard Morphet
Ms. Elizabeth A. Parr
Mr. and Mrs. Ted Paulissen
Miss Olga Peterson
Mr. Jack Porter
Mr. Leslie Radoff
Mr. and Mrs. Oscar Sarabia
Mrs. Mary Street Schoettle
Miss Teana Sechelski
Mr. and Mrs. George Strake
Mr. Louis Swilley
Tenneco, Inc.
Ms. Patricia Winkler
Mr. and Mrs. Frank Yeager
Miss Lois Young

Fr. William J. Young, C.S.B.

Contents

x

Contributors

THOMAS P. ADLER, an associate professor of English at Purdue University, has recently completed a critical study of the Pulitzer Prize-winning plays. He has published widely on modern British and American drama in such journals as *Arizona Quarterly, Comparative Drama, Modern Drama, Renascence,* and *Theatre Journal.* The essay included in this book brings to seven the number of book chapters, essays, and reviews which he has written on Albee.

MARY CASTIGLIE ANDERSON, an assistant professor of English at Lyman Briggs College/Michigan State University, has delivered several papers on the plays of Edward Albee and is author of "Staging the Unconscious: Edward Albee's *Tiny Alice*" in the journal, *Renascence.*

LEONARD CASPER, professor of creative writing and contemporary American literature at Boston College, is author/editor of eight volumes, including *Robert Penn Warren: The Dark and Bloody Ground; A Lion Unannounced,* a National Council of Arts short story collection; and *New Writing from the Philippines: A Critique and Anthology.* He has served on the editorial boards of *Literature East and West* and *Drama Critique.* His essays on Warren, Tennessee Williams, and Flannery O'Connor have appeared in anthologies.

PHILIP C. KOLIN, an associate professor of English at the University of Southern Mississippi, has written five books, including *Elizabethan Stage Doctor* and *Shakespeare in the South,* as well as numerous articles on drama, speech, and folklore which have appeared in such journals as *American Speech, The*

Explicator, Essays in Literature, and the *Shakespeare Newsletter.* Among his published works on Albee are three bibliographic pieces in *Serif* and *Resources for American Literary Studies* as well as an article on "The Bawdy Uses of Et Cetera" in *American Speech.*

CHARLES S. KROHN, a professor of English at The University of St. Thomas, has appeared in and/or directed nearly one hundred productions around the country, including featured roles in *The Three Sisters, Harvey, The Imaginary Invalid,* and Chayevsky's *Gideon* for Houston's Alley Theatre. His credits also include numerous appearances in both television and film.

VIRGINIA I. PERRY, a graduate assistant in English at the University of Colorado at Boulder, has published short stories and poetry. Her current research includes studies of the linguistic and epistemological themes in Albee's works.

LIAM O. PURDON, an assistant professor of English and American literature at Doane College, has published articles on Chekhov as well as on modern art. In addition to his work on Albee, he has delivered several papers on various aspects of medieval literature and is currently completing a study of short verse English romances.

MATTHEW C. ROUDANÉ, an assistant professor of English at Georgia State University, is currently completing a book on Albee. His work on the playwright includes a recently published interview in the *Southern Humanities Review.*

JULIAN N. WASSERMAN, an associate professor of English and linguistics at The University of St. Thomas, is co-author of *The Poetics of Conversion: Numerology and Alchemy in Gottfried's Tristan* as well as *Thomas Hardy and the Tristan Legend.* He is the author/co-author of numerous articles on medieval and modern literature appearing in such journals as *Neophilologus, Rice University Studies, Essays in Literature, Orbis Literarum,* and *The American Benedictine Review.*

EDWARD ALBEE

An Interview with Edward Albee
March 18, 1981

Charles S. Krohn and Julian N. Wasserman

Interviewer: I'd like to begin by asking you a few questions about your reputation as a playwright. The popular notion of Edward Albee is of a rather grim...

Albee: Grim and humorless.

Interviewer: Yes, grim and humorless. From the beginning you have been labeled an "angry" playwright. Yet from the beginning there has always been a great deal of humor, especially through word play, in your work. I wonder if you could account for the fact that so many people seem to have missed that aspect of your writing.

Albee: Maybe one of the reasons that I prefer Chekhov to Ibsen is that one thing Ibsen does not have is a sense of humor. You know, he's like Philadelphia: tell Ibsen a joke on Saturday, and he may laugh on Sunday, which is why you don't tell jokes in Philadelphia because you don't want people laughing in church. Humor — I've always thought that my plays were rather funny, and almost any work of art or play that has any merit or seriousness always has humor to it. I mean, well, there are exceptions. *Lear* isn't terribly funny. And I suppose there aren't too many jokes in *Oedipus Rex*—one or two. But most art has a sense of absurdity—the laughter in the dark, be it what you will. And God knows, you better have it in the twentieth century.

Interviewer: You use the term, "seriousness," in a number of your interviews. Could you define what you mean when you refer to "serious...."

1

Albee: ... as opposed to frivolous. ...

Interviewer: Yes, what do you mean by "serious drama"?

Albee: ... Opposite of frivolous. Engagement rather than escapist. Involved rather than uninvolved.

Interviewer: And by definition, engagement can't really take us into lighter realms?

Albee: I see no reason why it can't. Your true comedy which is not written by your gag writer—your true comedy is as instructive and useful as many other things.

Interviewer: *Virginia Woolf,* which a lot of people read as a very depressing play, seems to have a great deal of humor in it, again, especially the word play. Despite the fact that there is a great deal that is destructive about George and Martha, they seem quite admirable in many ways.

Albee: When I directed a revival in '76, I didn't change the play, the script, but I tried to emphasize the fact that George and Martha enjoyed their verbal duels with each other, and while they were deadly serious, they were always at the same time in admiration of each other's skills, and I wanted that to be clear. I wanted it to be clear that they were both using their minds very, very inventively throughout the play and that we could get some sense of the glee that they were having in what they were doing, and in that way reveal more of the humor of the piece. ... I always thought I was a droll playwright.

Interviewer: You do of course have a reputation as a very "active" artist, as one who not only writes and directs but who actively defends his work as well. Again, the popular notion of Edward Albee is that of a very outspoken writer who is a bit embattled by the critics.

Albee: Oh, I've given up on that.

Interviewer: What I was wondering was, when you describe yourself as being "with play," it's almost as if you were implying that the plays are your children. I wonder if that might not be a source of conflict. People can't be objective about their own children.

Albee: Oh yes, I can. No, of course, I use the concept of being "with play" merely to explain the genesis of each work ... that I'm not usually necessarily, specifically aware of the particular onset or occasion on which a play comes into being. It's really recreational rather than procreational thinking.

Interviewer: But you don't worry, then, that your being too close, too attached, to your plays could rob them of their craftsmanship?

Albee: No, it shouldn't. No, certainly not. My war with the critics was a misplaced war, I suddenly discovered a few years ago. But I used to complain that the critics were incompetent and that they served the public or the craft and art that they were criticizing particularly whether or not they were equipped to do it. Now I realize basically that it is up to newspapers and magazines to hire whatever level of incompetence they wish, and we have the protection of the Bill of Rights for this sort of thing, which permits incompetence almost everywhere in journalism. And the only problem was not with the stupidity of critics. That wasn't the major problem. The problem was basically in the fact of an audience or readership who assumed that what a critic said was a fact rather than a highly biased and quite often uninformed opinion and that you can't understand what a critic says unless you understand the mind of the critic and the limitations of the particular critic. And so it is the responsibility of people who read criticism to know whether they are reading the work of an ass or a man with some wisdom.

Interviewer: Since you're now engaged in college speaking tours, I would like to ask a few questions concerning how you think we should go about educating that audience or readership. It seems to me that you should have a fairly unique view of American education. In all of the biographical blurbs on your books and especially in your speech last night, you have stressed the fact that you were expelled first from several prep schools and later from Trinity University. Now you seem to have come full circle. You have taught drama at the university level and you are now engaged in college speaking tours.

Albee: I was most amused by my first honorary doctorate.

Interviewer: What do you think universities ought to be doing?

Albee: I don't think... my notions of education are so bizarre. As I said last evening, I think once a student has been informed how to educate himself and knows how to do that, then I think he has learned as much as he need learn in a formal educational structure unless he is going to go into the kind of employment where he has to have a degree. I think our colleges are cluttered with people who don't need to be there necessarily once they have learned how to educate themselves. And so, why should they clutter up the place? Leave it for people who need the degrees.

Interviewer: In *Seascape*, Charlie talks about what separates men from the animals. I think it's tools, art and a sense of one's own mortality. Do you think that an education should provide that?

Albee: All three. Yes. Certainly, of course.

Interviewer: Do you have any suggestions as to how we would go about providing those? Last night you seemed to argue that required courses are impediments rather than aids to education.

Albee: Look, there are a whole bunch of students who probably can't figure out how to educate themselves, ever. And I suppose they have got to be directed fairly carefully into some semblance of education. But there must be other students who, one can just see, should be allowed to pick and choose and take whatever courses are going to be useful to them because they understand how to educate themselves. So there should be, certainly, at least double standards.

Interviewer: Still though, if we are to educate the readership as you suggest, we have to teach, required or not. If you were given the task of introducing college freshmen to drama and decided to use one of your own plays, would any one come to mind as an obvious choice?

Albee: Well, the problem is that to introduce a freshman ... which I had to do once when I was teaching a semester at a city college in New York City during an open admission program where I found that my students had heard neither of drama nor of the theatre nor of words or thoughts for that matter, and I was to teach a survey course in twentieth century drama ... It occurred to me there was only one possible way to do it: Get all the films of plays that I could and all of the TV videotapes of drama that I possibly could and teach it as if it were a film course. And so there were only two of my plays that could fit into that sort of category—both *Virginia Woolf* and *A Delicate Balance*. And I chose *A Delicate Balance* because I thought it was a better film, a better representation of the play. I think that's a very useful way to teach students about drama: Show it to them from film; then get them to read it; then get them to see it on stage.

Interviewer: Yes, because it's the medium through which they get most of their information and experience anyway.

Albee: There's a superior production of *Uncle Vanya* that the Soviets made, by the way, with a Moscow art company. It's in Russian, but it's so extraordinary.

Interviewer: I haven't seen it. It's a shame that play is hardly ever done. Maybe that's because it is so difficult, but—to me—it's such a wonderful play.

Albee: It's my favorite of the Chekhov plays.

Interviewer: Any last thoughts on education?

Albee: Oh, I am worried, sometimes about the fact that there are so many students who are interested in Beckett and Genet and

Ionesco when they are in college and that ten years later, when they are out in what passes for the real world, the only plays they want to see are by Neil Simon.

Interviewer: Yes, that probably does happen, and, as you say, if there's no residual element still there ten years later....

Albee: I'm not so sure that it's only that. But I think there are pressures of community tolerance and lowering of standards that are deeply insidious, having to do with all of our advertising and most of our commercial entertainments, that are encouraging middle-browism and less as being standards of excellence. It's a miscomprehension of the democratic experience.

Interviewer: Have you given any thought to television writing as a means of trying to correct that "miscomprehension"?

Albee: You're talking contradictions.

Interviewer: You don't think it can be done, then?

Albee: I don't think that television's particularly interested in letting television drama be invented. It has to be invented since it's a different experience than writing for the stage or film. You can neither see nor hear on television, and so obviously it's got to be a totally different kind of drama that's written. But commercial television is not interested in that. Public television is too poor.

Interviewer: Simon Gray has written radio dramas.

Albee: Yeah, well in England that's quite a different matter. Everybody writes for television and for radio there. We have public radio here that nobody listens to. It was very interesting. I tried *Listening,* for a joint commission for the BBC and "Earplay" in this country. After it was performed on the radio, I received a whole package of reviews of the radio production from Britain—very perceptive, intelligent reviews. Not a one from the United States. I don't think anybody either reviewed it or maybe even listened to it.

Interviewer: I wonder if the problem of finding an audience doesn't have to do with the rarefied direction which serious drama has taken. I spoke to someone who saw *Lolita* in Boston, and he enjoyed it very much by the way. The man is a university professor and also a widely published poet, and the thing that struck me was that all of his comments were highly academic—about the process of adaptation and crossing over genres. They were, I guess, issues that would never really occur to the average theatre-goer—perhaps not even to a nonacademic critic. I wonder if the play hasn't found its audience and if that audience isn't a very elitist and therefore very small one?

Albee: With *Lolita*, I have a responsibility to those people who are bright enough to have read the book and understand its glories. But every play is appreciated by a different audience on a different level. There are some people who merely get the story line; there are people who get the implications of the story. There are yet others who can even attend to the language and listen to Nabokovian puns, whether they're Albeean puns which sound like Nabokovian puns or not. Everybody receives a different play, and also people who have read the book, *Lolita*, are going to bring their own ideal stage adaptation to it. Obviously, I will have done it differently. And they will not be quite as amused, maybe, as people who haven't read the book. I can't judge, of course, how anybody who hasn't read the book is going to respond to the play, since I have read the book more than once. But I can't conceive of everybody who's been seeing the play ... and we've been having full houses almost every night both in Boston and New York attending without previous ... God knows what will happen after we open. I can't imagine that everybody there has read the book since most people I have talked to have not read the book; they've only seen that awful film made from the book.

Interviewer: Still, you keep speaking of theatre as an informing, even shaping force in society. But then you maintain that the masses are unfamiliar with the backgrounds and are uneducated in their tastes. Can an art form without a mass following have any real effect on society, and isn't the type of "serious" drama of which you keep speaking really only the province of the few?

Albee: Well, only to the extent that a very small number of people go to the theatre. But I imagine there's a larger percentage of people who ultimately affect our society who go to the theatre than do not. We are supposed to be a democracy. But we know perfectly well that almost all of the decisions that the people are allowed to make have already been formulated and planned very carefully by one percent of one percent of one percent of the society. The choices that are permitted in the democratic process have already been limited. And I imagine that most of those people who are really making the choices in our theoretically democratic society are people who are affected by the theatre.

Interviewer: Again, it seems to me that all of this seems to point to a rather narrow concept of the people for whom you are writing.

Albee: I'm excluding people like presidents, of course, from this because those people are a result of what is being decided by this one percent of one percent of one percent, and most of our senators and representatives are too. Theatre must be an important shaping force. Why is it so many governments, when they decide to clamp down on freedom of expression, hit the theatre first? Because there is a real experience rather than a fantasy experience, I think.

Interviewer: But you do not see it then as an elitist form of art?

Albee: Not in intention. No, certainly not. But the dangers are clear here. So many playwrights — you watch them trying to reach a much larger audience than normally goes to the theatre. They coarsen; they cheapen; they lessen their work in order to broaden its appeal. One can work directly or indirectly. "Elitist" suggests that it is consciously created for an elite. I, not being much of an intellectual, find there's practically nothing in any of my plays that could not be comprehended by any ten people you want to take off the street here in Houston, if they are willing to go to the theatre and approach it open-mindedly.

Interviewer: To be honest—and this goes back to the professor who saw *Lolita* in Boston—the kinds of understanding and the perceptions that led to his enjoying the play were probably fundamentally different from those of the majority of the audience. I'm not sure that it's even fair to expect otherwise or maybe even to complain that it lacks an audience, whether on the radio or on stage. "Serious popular drama" may be contradiction in terms.

Albee: Yeah. But the play, *Lolita,* would have failed if it doesn't appeal, from my point of view, if it doesn't appeal to both audiences: the informed and the average theatre-goer. It must appeal to both. I don't write plays as an elitist act — in other words, only to appeal to a small number of people—though that seems quite often to be the result. So, when I write a play like *Quotations from Chairman Mao Tse Tung* or *Listening,* I realize that they are not going to reach the audience that *Virginia Woolf* or *A Delicate Balance* will. I'm quite aware of that. There's not much to be done about it. Just go about your business and do it.

Interviewer: It seems to me that the only people who are going to see a play like *Tiny Alice* are people who deliberately decide to see *Tiny Alice*—who decide to sit through it, and again this goes back to this idea of an elite audience. You can't seem to get a mass audience to tackle a play like that. I don't know what's to be done about that.

Albee: I don't know if there's anything to be done about it unless you educate an entire society into preferring Beckett to Neil Simon.

Interviewer: Do you think that that can be done or even should be done?

Albee: I think that participating in the arts and the life of the mind should be made a less disreputable occupation in this country—should be made something of a natural event, and I think that has to be done — oh goodness — by having your children listening to string quartets when they're four years old, impregnating them with all of this and looking at abstract pictures and reading books that are beyond them. I remember I was reading Turgenev when I was eight and a half. I found it in the library downstairs, and I loved it. It was wonderful. I don't know that I've read him since.

Interviewer: Speaking of Turgenev, do you see any merit to the theory that it is the public character of a play—that is where you have actors, the director, the audience, a kind of hodge-podge of contentiousness as opposed to the private character of the reading of a novel—that helps form, not perhaps the play itself, but "drama" in the larger sense?

Albee: I don't think so really. These imprecisions of the theatre don't really help us all terribly much. It's the way theatre is done. I would rather that a person who know how to read a play read a play of mine and see the performance in his head when he reads it than see a mediocre performance on stage. As opposed to many other people who feel that plays are complete only when they are performed, I am convinced that they are complete as a literary act which one can understand merely by reading. The performance is gravy, it seems to me: it's not the proof of the play.

Interviewer: Aristotle maintains the same things.

Albee: Does he?

Interviewer: He finally says that you can still get the catharsis of emotion only by reading the play as well as seeing it. Of course, that's comforting to teachers of plays. ... Let's consider the audience for a second. If the performance is not really necessary, how necessary is the audience?

Albee: Well, in my case, less and less. ... It depends upon your audience, of course. Now when a person reads a play, he's reading it by himself. I'm convinced he can have the complete experience of the play without having to be in the community of a lot of other people. ... Your informed reader is going to be doing exactly the same things as an audience is doing who is watching the play.

Interviewer: The play doesn't exist for its own sake, unread?

Albee: Well, obviously. ... no, it does. It's been written; therefore it exists. ... I have written; therefore, I am.

Interviewer: If we were to think of Nick and Honey as some sort of audience, or Peter in *The Zoo Story*, a number of characters like George and Martha or Jerry have a desire to exorcise themselves, so to speak. And they inevitably need someone to speak to, an audience.

Albee: Yes, of course they do.

Interviewer: It seems to me that *Virginia Woolf* would simply not be nearly so good a play without Nick and Honey as an onstage audience, as a barometer of the action. A three act argument between George and Martha, despite their wit, would not have worked as well.

Albee: Of course, George and Martha wouldn't be doing that without that particular audience.

Interviewer: In regard to *Virginia Woolf*, it has always seemed to me that much of the confusion in regard to the play is due to the theatre audience's misapprehension of the stage audience—that we are intended to see Nick and Honey critically instead of using them as merely a sounding board or seeing all of the action through their eyes. We should be watching Nick and Honey, in essence, to see how not to watch the play. The problem is that George and Martha are much more interesting and distract us.

Albee: People are going to relate to any play through the agency of whatever characters they can relate through. They are going to do it. The play you get in trouble with is when you don't give them any character to relate through. That's why they have some difficulty relating to Brecht quite often because his experiences are so completely different. That's fine with me so long as they have a character they can relate through. Better than not relating.

Interviewer: Does an audience have a right to have expectations of a playwright?

Albee: Yes, some expectations that the playwright write as well as he possibly can, tell as much truth as he knows, and do it as clearly as the complexity of the subject matter requires. And, of course, we who write feel that the audience has a kind of responsibility too — to be willing to have any kind of experience that the playwright can successfully deliver and not to predetermine the kind of experience one is willing to have and to come with a sufficiently open and alert mind that does not close down when there is disagreement on the stage with one's own views.

Interviewer: In other words, the function of the audience is to listen.

Albee: I've always thought the basic problem was not people's inability to understand, inability to relate, but a choice that's made, and you must not assume that, because they are not listening, that people cannot hear. You must assume that they don't hear. And you keep on talking because they may realize that they are not hearing by choice.

Interviewer: So that's why in *Listening* The Girl keeps saying, "you're not listening, you're not listening"?

Albee: Right.

Interviewer: Do you generally use surrogates in your plays? Is there ever one character, perhaps like The Girl in *Listening*, who speaks for you?

Albee: The danger there is that.... oh, you see so many plays by eager young playwrights. And somewhere along the third act, one character, usually a fairly major character who the author—who, if he's a 26-year-old guy, 5 feet 11 with brown hair—happens to put down in the directions "Tom, a sensitive, young composer, he switches it—brown hair, 5 feet 11 ...." And somewhere in the third act, this character delivers himself of a very long monologue explaining the play, the symbolism of the play and the author's thoughts, the author's anguish, and the author's intent in writing the play. These speeches should be removed from the play like any growth as soon as they possibly can. Surrogates: I'd like to think that I spread it out sufficiently so that nobody sees any character in there that is the author hammering away or yammering away.

Interviewer: And of course, I suppose the idea of any one character's possessing all of the truth seems a bit dogmatic, if not naive.

Albee: I think every character should be permitted to have some portion of the misunderstanding.

Interviewer: Yes, exactly. Shaw, as you know, was very fond of inserting spokesmen for his views in his plays. In fact, that leads to the next question. You mentioned the "usefulness" of the theatre, and you did, of course, discuss that to some extent. Shaw, for example, speaking of Ibsen's *The Doll's House*, says *A Midsummer Night's Dream* will be as fresh as new paint when *The Doll's House* will be as dull as dishwater. But he says *The Doll's House* in his estimation would have done more work, that it would have been more useful. It would have provided more instruction, more...

Albee: ...Social kinds of instruction. One of my problems with Ibsen is that he does seem bogged down to a certain extent with specifics that have very little resonance. Anything that does not resonate, doesn't send sparks off, seems to me less interesting. That's one of the reasons I prefer Chekhov to Ibsen in that particular area. But the usefulness of art in a more general sense has to do with the fact that it makes us understand consciousness and bring some order into the chaos of existence. That is the useful function of art — to direct our attention to a sense of rhythm, to a sense of order—to a comprehension of what it is to be, to be aware of oneself. That is the useful function of art. Art is not decorative unless it takes people away from this comprehension. Now, so much theatre is devoted, and almost all film and almost all television are devoted to taking people out of conscious awareness of themselves and putting them into a fantasy plane. Theatre does exactly the opposite. One of the reasons why people can sit in a movie and not be shocked by the sort of thing they are shocked at when they see it in a play is that they understand that the movie is a fantasy experience, and they understand that the play is a real experience.

Interviewer: Could you elaborate on that sense of rhythm and order that art brings to its audience?

Albee: ... I think there are a whole set of underlying biorhythms that probably control the nature of all the arts. I suspect there are some reasons why most string quartets are thirty minutes long and most plays are two hours. I think it has something to do with things other than commerce. I think it has to do with the cosmic breathing that we all do or some kind of collective unconsciousness. I'm not sure what. And so I'm sure there are these rhythms that determine that duration and intensity.

Interviewer: I've noticed when interviewers have asked you about "realism" and "naturalism" in your plays you've applied those terms even to your more abstract plays like *Tiny Alice* ...

Albee: ... And to all of Beckett's plays.

Interviewer: Do you mean that those plays are realistic in that they, through their non sequiturs and complex word-plays, in some sense capture those rhythms—the rhythms of thought?

Albee: Well, I hope they do. Be nice to think so.... I think there should also be in any interesting writing of drama at least three things going on at the same time. There is what is being said, what is not being said, the implications of what is not being said, and then there's the use of the character's interest and the use of language itself. ... And they should not necessarily even be falling in the same direction — these three things.

Interviewer: A moment ago, you spoke of "social kinds of instruction." That sounds like political drama, and, in fact, you've been called a political dramatist. How would you define "political drama"?

Albee: Two kinds. There's a kind of parochial, short term political drama—agitprop stuff that's maybe useful for a little while and

has absolutely no literary value to it whatever. Then there's a kind of more generalized political drama which realizes that it is the degree to which people are able to accept consciousness that justifies the degree to which they are permitted to participate in the consciousness that determines how they will govern themselves.

Interviewer: This comes back to—I think it was a quote in one of your interviews—your statement that you are more interested in the mentality of someone who would shoot John Kennedy than the actual moment of pulling the trigger.

Albee: Yes, it tells a good deal more about our society.

Interviewer: So, then this returns us to the idea that a play is a presentation of a state of mind on the stage.

Albee: Um hum. Mm Hmm.

Interviewer: Going back to your talk last night on the relationship between the arts and the political scene, or government, what precisely is that relationship? Is it that the art is a liberating force for the audience, for the readers?

Albee: It should be a teaching and liberating one. It should be. The resistance to so much that wishes to be teaching and liberating tells us as much about the health of our society as the acceptance does.

Interviewer: As long as we're on politics, do you see yourself as an "American" playwright, in particular a playwright in a distinctly American tradition?

Albee: Well, I'm American. I travel a lot around the world, but I daresay that my perceptions are from growing up in this country. I'm sure they are.

Interviewer: Anything in particular that you see as peculiarly American about your art?

Albee: Well, I'm certainly not a regional American writer, unless you want to consider Westchester County outside of New York a region. And I don't think it is. It's a state of mind very much like Palm Springs and Palm Beach and places like that...and Newport. These are not places. I'm not a regionalist. But I think I'm more American than European as a writer.

Interviewer: How so?

Albee: Well, I must be since all of my perspectives have been formed by growing up and living in this particular society and standing to one side of it. Maybe I'm sort of mid-Atlantic.

Interviewer: It struck me last night when you were talking about your traveling for the state department as an American artist...I wondered if there was something in particular that you represented. If you were in the Soviet Union and someone said, "OK, you're an American artist — what does that mean," how would you answer a question like that?

Albee: I never go around introducing myself as an "American" playwright. I don't do it. I don't go around introducing myself, period. But if they want to attach that label to me, it's more accurate than "Lithuanian" playwright, you know. I'm a playwright from America. I do not have corn tassels behind my ear and shit on my boots.

Interviewer: Can we get your vision of America?

Albee: No! You mustn't ask anyone who spends most of his time in New York City for his vision of the United States.

Interviewer: That's a pretty separationist view, especially for the author of *The American Dream.*

Albee: No, I do spend a lot of time traveling around this country and I've learned far more about it in the last seven or eight years than I ever knew before.

Interviewer: Any comment on the "American" family?

Albee: (laugh)...Wait until the next play....The next play will probably be called "Quitting." And that takes your average American upper-middle-class family: husband, wife, daughter, son-in-law ... their grandmother, perhaps.

Interviewer: The old crowd...there is always a grandmother.

Albee: And even the grandfather. The old crowd but handling quite different matters.

Interviewer: Any children in it so far?

Albee: This girl, about twenty-two.

Interviewer: No. That's a little older than I meant. Any *young* children? Families seem to be a favorite topic, and yet there don't seem to be any children about. In that regard, I thought that the choice of *Lolita* was interesting because it seems to me that that was going to be your first attempt at portraying a child.

Albee: I've got a fifteen-year-old — fourteen-and-a-half — in *Everything in the Garden.*

Interviewer: Well, you've got me there. Still, that too is an adaptation, and....

Albee: Also, you know, you can't give many lines to child actors. And *Lolita* is being played by a twenty-four-year-old girl. There are two things to keep off stage if you're doing a serious play: children and dogs....You put a dog on stage, people only watch the dog. Put a child on stage, people listen to the child. The child can't carry a message very well....In *A Delicate Balance,* the daughter, whatever her name is.

Julia, has no kids. However, who is to say that the son in *All Over,* he has a wife... I'm sure he's got some kids offstage somewhere. I don't clutter up the stage with prop actors.

Interviewer: But the onstage family relationships are very interesting. The family members always seen to be cut off from each other. That brings us to a touchy question. Your average critic, at least the academic one, reads the play and says—"Let's see. Here's a fellow who was adopted, and he doesn't put kids on stage." Then he starts making biographical correspondences, which I understand you don't care for. How important is your biography in understanding your work?

Albee: Biography and me? Oh, I think totally unimportant. It seems to infuriate some scholars that they can't pin everything down because I tend to be a fairly private person. There is very little in my life that is of such great apparent significance or of earth-shaking importance that would lead to this or that play. And I'd rather people judge the work for itself rather than by biographical attachments. I don't know what good it does. I think maybe it makes us misunderstand more than understand.

Interviewer: And that's why Auden willed that all his letters be burned?

Albee: Yeah. You just see what happens about that. I am always bothered when I am informed too much about the author of something that I have admired. In the same way, when I listen to opera, I'm more interested in listening to the music than I am in knowing what's going on in the story. And I'm very upset when I hear an opera in English, for that very reason. What does it matter what the private lives of people are? Quite often the private lives of people are boring and niggardly little events leading to something pretty glorious in literature. Let's ignore the events so that we can concern ourselves with the piece itself. No worthwhile piece of literature is any good if it has to be related to some biographical factor in the author's life.

Interviewer: Yet with a lot of modern artists, the first thing that people ask for is a biography. Perhaps that's because so many writers write only in their own idiolects about their own experiences. The artist ends up as a type of "hunger artist" making art out of himself.

Albee: Well, one is always making art out of oneself. The art is the interesting thing, not the carcass.

Interviewer: If your work is not, then, autobiographical, is it, at least, based on your experiences?

Albee: I imagine that every writer writes from a whole complex of things. From things that happened, things he pretends have happened, people he's known, himself, and invention and creativity. He puts it all together. The function of writing is to turn fact into truth. And so facts are not terribly important aside from what they can lead to.

Interviewer: I'd like to follow up with a few more questions about how it is that you go about your writing. Does a sense of dissatisfaction with the work just completed drive you towards your next effort, or are you simply moving in different directions with the next play?

Albee: Well, I suspect that all writers like to think that they can improve their craft each time. I don't know that I feel any extraordinary sense of dissatisfaction when I finish a work. I suspect that I have a sense of perhaps this work will not emerge to be quite as glistening as I thought it was because I probably fall a little short of my intention each time. But my mind fills with plays, and I write them down from time to time to unclutter my mind. As to whether or not there is some kind of structure or order to what I do, and there may well be, I don't spend very much time examining it. The whole concept of dissatisfaction is what I think drives the creative writer to his, well, back in the 14th century to his plume and these days to his IBM ... dissatisfaction with the way things are. In a utopian society, we'd have no literature, no art, because there would be no need for any, because all art is corrective.

Interviewer: I'd like, with fair warning, to ask a loaded question here. A number of your characters who, as artists of a sort, feel a desperate need to speak, to express themselves, and when they do participate in this sort of necessary exorcism, it is always a very painful experience.

Albee: Well, I suspect that a cheerful exorcism, or an exorcism without any discomfort, is probably not a particularly profound exorcism.

Interviewer: OK. Now, here's the loaded part of that. When you talk about your own writing, your own career, you don't seem to talk about suffering very much. You did have your first play put on rather quickly. You were an immediate success, shortly after turning to playwriting.

Albee: Whose suffering do I not talk about?

Interviewer: Your own suffering.

Albee: My own, or the characters' suffering? My own suffering; what suffering?

Interviewer: It seems to me that you describe writing as a fairly easy act: "uncluttering the mind"—something very different from what your characters go through in order to express themselves.

Albee: It's a very involving act for me. It creates a reality far more intense than what other people are thinking of as reality while I am doing it. Painful? No. It's hard work and exhilarating at the same time. After all, I could never write a play in the middle of anguish myself. We writers... that lovely poet Frank O'Hara said—we write in memory of our feelings. And the only way a person can write effectively about anything that is highly charged emotionally is to be able to objectify it, to transfer it to a character and let the character have that emotion. Unless you do that particular kind of objectification, then you are incapable of being in control of the emotional content of what you're doing.

Interviewer: You seem to be very much in the Romantic tradition: "Recollection in tranquility," as Wordsworth put it.

Albee: Well, not necessarily tranquility. Recollection, of course. At least getting far enough away from it so that one can give order to the experience. Otherwise, if you write about present tense emotions, you're suffering a feeling yourself; it's just going to slide all over the page and not have any order or structure. So that's why you write in memory of your feelings. So that pain, whatever pain, to answer your question.... I am circuitous, as you may have noticed.

Interviewer: You don't have to run upon someone's knife, then, like Jerry in *The Zoo Story*?

Albee: No, not I, no. I certainly have to be able to translate that into the characters' emotions.

Interviewer: Concerning this ability: supposing you suddenly found that you had lost it. The popular concept of the artist is of a maker, of a creator. It seems as though an artist has to maintain his productivity if he is to maintain the adulation of the public.

Albee: Well, if you're interested in maintaining adulation. I don't know if that is an honorable goal at all.

Interviewer: Again, if for argument's sake you arbitrarily decided never to write another play and simply walked around as Edward Albee, educated man and author of the plays you've already written, it would seem to me that a lot of people would no longer consider you an artist.

Albee: The universities are filled with people who are walking around as educated men rather than doing creative acts ... of that specific sort. Universities, a lot of them, are filled with ex-composers, ex-painters, ex-writers, who are teaching these crafts. I write only because I have ideas in my head and I want to get them out of my head. I daresay, I'd like to think when I stop having ideas, I'll stop writing.

Interviewer: This notion of the artist as creator leads to the question of adaptations. There seems to be a popular prejudice against adaptations. We seem to expect our artists to create *ex nihilo*. I've read a number of critics who say that the movement to adaptation is a sure sign of waning powers.

Albee: I don't know why. I have no idea why. It's an honorable craft.

Interviewer: Adaptation seems to be a natural outgrowth of what you have frequently described as your method of writing by coming to live with a character such that you can put him into random situations and predict his reactions. Aren't you doing the same thing only with other writers' characters?

Albee: If you find something congenial to your own point of view, then your adaptation of it becomes far closer to what you would have done, although you've merely taken someone else's plot which is congenial to your mind and are using it, so it's not a lesser task at all, it seems to me.

Interviewer: In regard to your adaptation of *Lolita*, what "improvement" do you hope to make with *Lolita*? In other words, I guess what I'm asking really is what, if you can generalize about this, is the effect of dramatizing a nondramatic piece of literature?

Albee: It translates it from one medium to another. It's a fundamental translation, and one must not try to be literal; one must do equivalencies. You may get into an experience that seems to belong completely on the stage—one that is going to be satisfying to somebody who's never read the book and also someone who has.

Interviewer: I've heard French teachers, people whose native language is French, say that Bryan Hooker's translation of *Cyrano* is to many of them superior to the original play. On the other hand, read some of those awful turn-of-the-century type of translations of *Cyrano*. Instead of Hooker's lines of, "your name is like a bell hung in my heart, and when it rings I tremble," and so on, you actually get the literal translation such as "your name is like a clapper in the bell when it bangs against the side of the bell."

Albee: An ideal translation does find equivalencies, of course. Sometimes they're absurd ones, but when they did *Who's Afraid of Virginia Woolf?* in Prague, they changed the title to *Who's Afraid of Franz Kafka?* and things like that. And there is a delicate line between creative translation and excessive adaptation too. But I would rather, I suppose, have a bit of excessive adaptation than literalness—"the clapper of the heart."

Interviewer: The term "translation" seems to crop up in both a number of your plays and interviews. You seem unusually interested in language—not just in the act of translating ideas from one language to another, or even in terms of what you have called "Albeean puns," but in the process of translation, if I may use the term, of ideas into words. *Counting the Ways* appears to be an elaborate exercise in semantics. In terms of a formal interest in linguistics and semantics, could I ask if you've done a lot of reading in linguistic theory? Is that an interest of yours?

Albee: Yes, but I find some of the books on linguistic theory incomprehensible. The greatest fun I ever had, of course, was with Lancelot Hogben's *Whip the Mother Tongue,* which was a great deal more fun to me than reading the French linguistic philosophers, for example.

Interviewer: I notice that the term "semantics" comes up in a number of plays.

Albee: Quite often pejoratively.

Interviewer: That seems to reflect a very specifically Zen attitude towards language. Much of your dialogue seems to be very like the Zen Koan. You have Charlie quote one Koan in *Seascape,* as a matter of fact. At any rate, your attitude towards the limitations of language seems very oriental.

Albee: Well, I wouldn't be surprised. It sounds interesting, and it sounds pretty good, and so I will take to it.

Interviewer: Tallyrand was reported as saying that man invented language in order to avoid meaning. . . .

Albee: That was French.

Interviewer: Along those lines, we have the example, say, of Beckett, whose plays quite obviously are moving in the direction of silence. If language is unreliable, as you seem to indicate it is, is that trend a good thing or a dead end?

Albee: Well, silence, of course, is a dead end. And you may have noticed that Beckett is edging *slowly* towards silence. I would imagine he will take another fifteen plays before he gets there. By that time, his career will be over. He will be dead. But the importance of silence as well as sound is something that, again, we get from Chekhov, as much as from anybody, and Beckett following through, though I sometimes think there's a relationship to that and the highly organized structure of sound and silence in Greek plays, for example. It's something that we miss out on, a whole area of the history of drama. And maybe it was something Chekhov got from the Greek dramatists; I'm not sure. There is a whole formalization of rhythms which is similar in its effect to sound and silence. People, indeed, do use a lot of this to avoid meeting quite often. But a playwright, of course, has the responsibility and the use of language, and silence is merely another weapon of language.

Interviewer: And of course, I think in many of your plays — I think you might agree — that many of the characters are shown using language as this very mask....

Albee: Using it at great lengths to avoid communication. Talk and so...in order not to have to listen.

Interviewer: I've noticed that a number of times your characters say something like "I'm going to speak to you in your own language," and yet they never really seem able to do that. Linguistic misunderstanding seems to be an important part of your dialogue.

Albee: Well, I can't resist if somebody says something that has a ramification. I can't resist digressing to the ramification because it's so much fun.

Interviewer: I love that scene in *Seascape* where Charlie and Leslie are arguing about the difference between a foot and a hand. I think that's a great scene.

Albee: I enjoyed writing it as I recall.

Interviewer: That and I guess the linguistic bartering over "wheat" and "beige" in *The American Dream*. Well, I guess I will stoop to symbol-mongering here. The lunch box in that play has always seemed an apt metaphor for what I believe is your concept of language. Mommy knows what is inside it. She deliberately lets others misunderstand what she means when she says it's too pretty to be opened. People on one end of the speech act understand words to mean one thing; people at the other end believe it to be something else.

Albee: Sure, *The American Dream* to a large extent was about the rapid breakdown of communication. People just don't listen. That's why Mommy was able to say to Mrs. Barker, "won't you take off your dress" rather than "won't you take off your coat." And one doesn't listen and doesn't pay attention.

Interviewer: That is the point of *Listening*, I suppose?

Albee: Yes, to a large extent.

Interviewer: *Listening* appears to be an extended epistemological exercise — almost in the tradition of the medieval *psychomachia*. I keep finding in it metaphors for the linguistic process, for what happens when we speak—the grey cardboard painted blue, for instance. It's not grey cardboard; it's not blue cardboard in the same way that words are neither the ideas that generate them nor the objects they represent. The same is true for the play itself. It's not an action; it's an imitation. At the same time it is not the pure idea in the mind of the playwright either.

Albee: You want a job as a critic for *The New York Times*?

Interviewer: Certainly, I'd love it.

Albee: I'll see if I can arrange it.

Interviewer: Seriously, here I am blithely explaining to you what I think your work is all about in terms of grey cardboard and all. How do you react to that kind of exegesis of your work?

Albee: Well, you didn't notice my eyes glazing over as you said it because I thought it was fairly intellectually stimulating, and so I was interested by it—true if truly interesting. I have read definitions of what I have attempted in certain plays that make me think that they've obviously read the plays of someone else. And I've come across others that correspond to my notion of what I've probably intended, and I find those a lot more interesting. But I can't take myself seriously enough to read all these books about me with a great degree of absorption.

Interviewer: And academic studies. How do you feel about books that purport to explain your works?

Albee: Mildly amused, Yeah, I'm always puzzled at people who can do it... I read these books about me. I'm sent numbers of copies of books about me and scholarly papers, and I read them the way I do fiction. There was this writer....

Interviewer: Do you find that, in general, people discuss your plays very intelligently with you?

Albee: No.

Interviewer: Why do you think that is?

Albee: I don't think people should go around trying to discuss art intelligently with each other.

Interviewer: Specifically plays or just art in general?

Albee: When you get together with a bunch of people in New York who are painters and writers, you don't sit around discussing aesthetics. You don't do it. You talk about which way the good restaurant is, and you talk about money and sex and food the way everybody else does. You don't go around talking about writing or painting. Every once in a while, you know, "Hey, that's a good painting—glad to see that you suddenly started to shape your canvas;" then you go back to something important.

Interviewer: On the other hand, if a play is supposed to do what you seem to want it to do — make your audience react, think, respond — is it natural that somebody in your audience would turn to somebody else and say, "I saw this play or I read this play, and it interested me," would....

Albee: Yes, of course, and they don't have to go around explaining and intellectualizing why the play interested them. If this was interesting, go see it. If people want to talk about something they've experienced, that's fine.

Interviewer: I can appreciate the dangers inherent in those kinds of formulations. Let's go from my intellectualizing to yours. Do you think that giving interviews like this has affected your art? Do you think that there is a danger in objectifying the creative process?

Albee: The only virtue of giving interviews and answering questions in a situation of this sort, or any situation, is that quite often you do have to articulate, perhaps for the first time, some things that you had been thinking about, and every once in a while you slip and inform yourself that you've come to a conclusion about something you weren't aware of having come to. And that's interesting.

Interviewer: Obviously, then, you feel that you can separate your role as an artist from that as a critic.

Albee: Oh yes. Every time I write a play, it's as though it's the first play that not only I have written, but it's the first play that anybody has written. And I spend most of my life filling myself with outside influences and stimuli. Though when I'm writing a piece, I have to empty my mind of every single thing except technical control and the fact that Edward is inventing the drama.

Interviewer: And so it's not a problem that at one place you say good drama is such and such and that the next time you sit down to write a play you are a prisoner of your own definition?

Albee: No. My plays vary so much from one to the other in method and style and direction that I can't concern myself with any of that.

Interviewer: Concerning that variety of style and method, I've heard you compared to O'Neill in the sense that O'Neill kept changing and experimenting to the point that every time people thought they understood what he was up to, he struck out in a different direction and left them baffled.

Albee: Well, maybe O'Neill did it on purpose. I don't do it on purpose. I'm interested in the fact that I write plays in such different styles from time to time. Different degrees of abstraction, that interests me. I'm not doing it to avoid, or to revenge, or to confuse, or to be fresh in my mind, even. I just do it because that is the way each one wants to be.

Interviewer: Do you see anything that they have in common?

Albee: No (Headshake).

Interviewer: Most writers seem to have a common theme. Do you feel that you have themes that are re-worked?

Albee: I suppose maybe in the same way Chekhov has. What are Chekhov's themes? Examining the slow side of the decline of his society leading up to the revolution. Very few Russian writers besides Turgenev and Chekhov spoke of what was going to happen in 1917 more clearly. One of Chekhov's concerns beyond that was people who let things go, people who do not speak, people who avoid rather than comfront. But I think I may have learned a lot from Chekhov. I certainly hope I have.

Interviewer: If someone were to look at your entire corpus, would it be possible to abstract a definition of what drama means to Edward Albee—in other words an Albeean concept of a play?

Albee: I don't really know that I can do that. I can't bring myself to think about my work in those terms. I just can't do it. And also, I've written... what... nineteen plays out of the forty or so that I plan to write. And maybe when I am at the end of it, I may be able to say something comprehensive about the overall shape of it. But at this point, no. I just go on. I've got five plays in my head right now. One of them is about Atilla the Hun, by the way, and four of them are not.

Interviewer: Is is true, then, that the artist is the worst person to go to for an interpretation of a work? Would you agree with the artist who answers questions about meaning by handing you the play and saying, "Well just read the play. That's what I meant"?

Albee: Who said, "A poem is, and it means what it says"? I've discovered over the years that the most interesting reactions that I get to my work are from other people in the arts. Not necessarily from other playwrights—but from composers, and painters and poets—that I get a far more useful, to me, reaction to my work from these people, which may be part of the elitist thing—that we are writing for a small crowd of people who understand us. I don't think it's true. I just think people who do or are involved in the arts can bring to the arts a unique comprehension of them, and that's why they should be critics rather than these people who are not involved in the arts being hired as critics.

People involved in the arts do bring something to an understanding of other arts that older people don't bring — a community of creativity perhaps that leads to an understanding of intention very, very nicely. I keep asking newspapers and magazines, why don't you hire creative people as critics? You get informed prejudice that way rather than uninformed prejudice.

Interviewer: So you object to people who are unable to create writing about those who do. Can't criticism itself be a creative act?

Albee: Well, I'm not talking about failed people. I'm talking about Robert Rauschenberg, the poetry critic here, and I should criticize the reviews of painting and sculpture, which I do. I find myself doing an awful lot of writing. I've written many essays and curated exhibits of painting and sculpture. I'm getting more and more involved in that because I think that... I am told, and I agree to a certain extent, I bring to writing about painting and sculpture attitudes that only a writer can bring to them—somebody else involved in the arts. And they tell the person who's made the art something about their practice of their own craft, something that somebody who is not in the creative arts can't bring. I think I kept all of the negatives proper in that sentence. It was getting a little tricky there toward the end.

Interviewer: You managed to save yourself. James Thurber said once that Hemingway got lost in a "which" clause one time but that he was able to recover because he was a young, healthy man.

Albee: Why does nobody read Thurber anymore?... God, he's a funny writer and a serious one at the same time, at his very best. I've learned a great deal from Thurber, by the way—his sense of absurdity — a marvelous writer. I love his story, I think it was "The Waters of the Moon," in which he was writing about a visit he made to a writer named Douglas Bryce, who was having that crisis collapse of his career in the fifties—in his early fifties—when he reached fifty and decided that he was going to finally make a breakthrough—he can always write a trilogy. And so he wrote it on his bathroom mirror—"the mountain, the plain, the sea—a trilogy by Douglas Bryce." And then Thurber writes, "But he was onto himself because underneath it all, he had scribbled, a trilogy-wilogy by Brycey-Wycey." Thurber's one of our best stylists, as a matter of fact.

Interviewer: Along with Thurber and Chekhov, whom you've already mentioned, what writers have influenced your own writing?

Albee: Who has influenced me?... I'm reported to have said at one time ... sometime in the past when the question about my influences ... I implied that I was influenced by Socrates and Noel Coward,

which is indeed true. And I would imagine quite a number of people in
between. We should be influenced by everything we experience in the
art—the bad and the good. I think people who only attend masterpieces
are probably not understanding the nature of the art these masterpieces are done in. You must learn from what people have done badly
as well as from what people have done well. And God knows that in
commercial theatre there's plenty of opportunity. You learn as much,
maybe even more, from other people's errors than you do from the
other people's successes.

Interviewer: I think so. It's about as easy, I suppose, to criticize
a bad play as a good play.

Albee: And so, any teacher ... when he's teaching literature,
should teach half bad and half good. He merely must have instructed
his students to know which is which.

Interviewer: Could we turn the previous question around?
Where do you see your own influence?

Albee: I don't know the answer to any question of that sort.
Sometimes somebody says to me, "Oh, you must see this play off
Broadway; it's very influenced by you." And so, I'll go and look at it, and
I can't find the influence. I can't possibly tell what it is. I don't think
about myself in the third person. I don't examine the nineteen plays
that I've done so far to see whether they make any coherent statement
or what direction they are pointing in, and I don't concern myself with
any of that. I think it's unwise for a writer to.

Interviewer: Then the directions or statements, if they exist,
are unconscious. A good deal of your writing seems to be on that level.
You frequently describe the process of writing as simply living with the
pieces of a puzzle until they fall into place. Do you ever feel any guilt
over having these ideas just pop up?

Albee: No, none whatever. Why should I?

Interviewer: I'm not saying you should. I have known writers
who have said that they weren't sure where their ideas come from,
especially poets, and they're successful, but they feel a little defensive in
that it's as though some blessing has fallen upon them.

Albee: No. The thing that differentiates creative people from
non-creative people is merely a different kind of access to the subconscious; that's all.

Interviewer: Do you see that as something which isolates you
or separates you from everybody else?

Albee: Mmmmm yeah, plus this ability to objectify an experience one is in.

Interviewer: Please don't be offended, but since this ability is one that separates the artist from the rest of the community, would you describe yourself as lonely?

Albee: No!

Interviewer: You would not?

Albee: I have never been lonely in my life. I prefer a certain amount of aloneness from time to time, but I've never been lonely.

Interviewer: Again, this comes back to the idea of what seems to happen in many of the plays to characters who are sensitive. That intellectual sensitivity seems to make them freaks. They seem very alone.

Albee: In the general society, yes. But I think all creative people are slightly to one side of their society—slightly outside of it. If they were in the mainstream of it, they wouldn't be in any position to comment upon it.

Interviewer: Their intellect, then, cuts them off. Have we strayed into elitism again?

Albee: No. It doesn't cut them off. It makes them aware that there are so many implications—more implications to everything that is being done and said than other people are.

Interviewer: You don't see that kind of awareness as a curse in that sense?

Albee: Oh, I don't find any curse. I'm fascinated by the fact that I can be very much involved in something and at the same time be aware that I'm observing myself in it. From a writer's point of view, I don't find that diminishes the experience. It just refracts it.

Interviewer: Truman Capote, when he was doing the talk shows following the publication of *Music for Chameleons,* was talking about writing. He said he could not think of a major American writer, I think he was speaking of prose writers, who wasn't a drunkard.

Albee: I know an awful lot of them do drink.

Interviewer: Do you think there's a reason for that? Again we have this association: The Romantic concept of the artist who suffers and is somehow set apart from the rest of society.

Albee: Well, there are some people who can't take the disloca-tion. What we were talking about, the ability to objectify, some people find that terribly difficult to deal with. And also a lot of writers get terribly involved in the old brass ring game.

Interviewer: Which would be?

Albee: The need to publish or perish, the need for the adula-tion, the need for the public awareness. And they get destroyed by it, a lot of them. . . . By the way, I know fewer playwrights who are drunks than novelists. Many more novelists are drunks than playwrights . . . interesting.

Interviewer: No comment on . . .

Albee: I mean, you think of famous drunks in twentieth century American letters, you have Thurber; you have Cheever; you have O'Hara; you have Hemingway; you have Fitzgerald. When you go back, you've got an awful lot of drunks. But how many of our playwrights are drunks?

Interviewer: Capote described his writing as an act of saving himself from his drunkenness and the pain of it all. Again, I could see that in a lot of your characters, but I could not see that in you.

Albee: It's quite possible there's some of the chemical imbalances in a writer's mind, the same chemical imbalances that create creativity—electrical and chemical imbalances. Maybe the same chemical imbalances that lead to alcoholism, to schizophrenia and various other things.

Interviewer: You're very interested in science aren't you?

Albee: Especially the mind.

Interviewer: I guess that comes back to the epistemological aspects of your work. Your point about the chemistry of the mind reminds me of The Girl's electro-chemical description of the brain in *Listening*.

Albee: Mm Hmm.

Interviewer: I can see that we're beginning to wind down here, Perhaps we should end up with something completely out of left field. If you'll excuse the non sequitur, do you lie during your interviews? (Pause) . . . Well . . . do you at least fool yourself?

Albee: That's quite a different matter. I'm sure I do fool myself from time to time. I think it is unwise for any person to go around thinking he doesn't fool himself at least two-thirds of the time. I don't necessarily consciously lie. Quite often I do things to amuse myself and which will run contrary to conclusions that people have come to from what I've said before.

Interviewer: I mean when you look me in the eye and glibly say, "Well, I'm not an intellectual," I can't help but wonder . . .

Albee: There're degrees of intellectualism here. I'm not one of your people who can be terribly coherent about thoughts. I assume that intellectuals are supposed to be able to do that. I'm a fairly well informed person and reasonably bright, but I don't claim to be an intellectual.

Interviewer: At the same time, I get the feeling, and I don't mean this in a strictly pejorative way, that you frequently have the experience of being the most intelligent person in the room.

Albee: I try to avoid that. I'm upwardly mobile.

"The Pitfalls of Drama"
The Idea of Language in the Plays of Edward Albee[1]

Julian N. Wasserman

I N RESPONSE to an interviewer's question concerning the supposed lack of "realism" in his work, Edward Albee noted the implicit contradiction between the nature of drama as imitation, in the Aristotelian sense, and the expectation of realism on the part of a play's audience.[2] The importance of this argument is that such a recognition goes far beyond the aesthetics of drama and touches upon the symbolic, that is imitative, nature of language—a problem that is frequently at the thematic heart of Albee's works.[3] Indeed, the common thread that runs through many of his seemingly diverse plays is his characters' oft-stated concern with language and, in particular, the failures and limitations of the linguistic medium. For Albee, language is the medium or meeting ground which exists between the interior and exterior worlds of the speaker and the listener. As a playwright, he seems most interested in the function of language as a means of translating ideas into actions and in the role of language as mediator where a word, like a play, is an imitation which is a wholly independent sign, distinct and separate from that which it represents. As such, a word, like any piece of drama, is neither a pure idea of an action or event nor the event itself. In essence, the naming done by the semanticist and the storytelling practiced by the playwright are, for Albee, congruent if not identical actions.

The problematical nature of language is succinctly set forth in *Seascape* during an argument between Charlie and Nancy in the opening

scene of the play. The practical onset of the debate is Charlie's use of the
past rather than present perfect tense, and as so often happens in the
works of Albee, the linguistic bartering over a particular term quickly
evolves into a more general and abstract debate over the nature and
function of language:

> Nancy: Do you know what I'm *saying?*
>
> Charlie: *You're throwing it up to me; you're telling me I've had a ...*
>
> Nancy: *No-no-no! I'm saying what you said, what you told me.* You told
> me, you said to me, "You've had a good life."
>
> Charlie: *(Annoyed.)* Well, you have! You *have* had!
>
> Nancy: *(She, too.)* Yes! Have *had!* What *about* that!
>
> Charlie: What about it!
>
> Nancy: *Am* not *having. (Waits for reaction; gets none)* Am not *hav-
> ing?* Am not *having* a good life?
>
> Charlie: Well, of *course!*
>
> Nancy: Then why say had? Why put it that way?
>
> Charlie: It's a way of speaking!
>
> Nancy: No! It's a way of thinking! *I* know the language and I
> know *you.* You're not careless with it, or didn't used to be.
> Why *not* go to those places in the desert and let our heads
> deflate, if it's all in the past? Why not just *do* that?
>
> Charlie: It was a way of speaking.
>
> Nancy: Dear God, we're *here.* We've served out time, Charlie and
> there's nothing telling us to do *that,* or any conditional;
> not any more. Well, there's the arthritis in my wrist, of
> course, and the eyes have known a better season, and
> there's always the cancer or a heart attack to think about if
> we're bored, but besides all these things... what is there?
>
> Charlie: *(Somewhat triste.)* You're at it again.
>
> Nancy: I am! Words are lies; they *can* be, and you *use* them, but I
> know what's in your gut. I *told* you, didn't I?[4]

The problem, then, is that language, while it is the figurative medium
through which Charlie is expressing the feelings in his "gut," is merely a
symbol for those feelings and may, by nature, serve to obscure rather
than to reveal them. As Nancy notes, her understanding of Charlie's
meaning is intuitive rather than linguistic and is based first on her
knowledge of Charlie and, second, on her understanding of the nature

of language. Furthermore, an important part of the argument out of which these linguistic considerations arise is devoted to Charlie's and Nancy's discussion of their sexual fantasies, or as Nancy terms it, the problem of "when the real and the figurative come together" (p. 23). Remarkably, the discussion of these sexual imaginings which Nancy describes as "the sad fantasies, the substitutions, the thoughts we have" (p. 25) culminates in Nancy's discovery that Charlie's fantasy was to "pretend that I was me" (p. 25), thus again presenting the attempt to join the intangible product of the inner man with that which is experienced in the world of phenomena. Described in slightly different— though still in a combination of philosophical, linguistic and sexual terms—the same desire is expressed by The Man in *Listening:* "Odd, in retrospect: it's such a thing we all want—though we seldom admit it, and when we *do,* only part; we all wish to devour ourselves, enter ourselves, be the subject and the object all at once; we all love ourselves and wish we could."[5] The goal is to make subject and object, idea and form, identical, and the pronouncement is immediately followed by a short interval of linguistic "bargaining" over The Man's use of the word "take."

Furthermore, the conversation containing sexual fantasies which appears at the beginning of *Seascape* contains a likewise significant discussion in which Charlie and Nancy compare the difference between their memories of days past and their perceptions of their less pleasant present. Finally, the opening dialogue contains Nancy's suggestion that Charlie attempt to recapture those days, or make memory and fact one, by re-enacting his childhood act of holding stones and sinking to the bottom of the sea in order to escape, if only for a moment, the chaos of the world above. This, of course, all serves as a prelude to the face to face confrontation between the humans and their reptilian counterparts. As the dialogue between the beings from, in their own words, two different dimensions might suggest, the conjunction between the real and the ideal is clearly the central theme of the play.[6]

As the lines from *Listening* suggest, the playwright's concern with the relationship between idea and actuality is certainly not limited to *Seascape.* The same nominalistic exploration is most elaborately set forth in the abstract in *Tiny Alice* with its butler named "Butler," a symbolic precursor of the joining of the real and the figurative in Charlie's sexual fantasies. The originally intended title of the earlier play, "Substitute Speaker," and its use of Alice as a substitute or proxy for the "Abstract" in the marriage to Julian further suggest a

connection with the "substitutions" of which Nancy speaks in the discussion of fantasy. The same theme is no less forcefully, though a good
deal less obliquely, presented in the battle over "Truth and Illusion" in
Who's Afraid of Virginia Woolf?. It is there that the illusionary is made
real in the imaginary son and that the real is made illusion in George's
"autobiographical" novel. Thus while Albee has enjoyed a reputation
as an innovator whose constant experimentation has, to some, robbed
his work of a clear and consistent stylistic voice, his plays have for the
most part maintained a consistency of thematic concern. Significantly,
most of those concerns will be seen to be the natural outgrowths or even
elaborations of the material of his first play.

In *The Zoo Story*, the theme of the disparity between idea and
experience is again presented in regard to sexual fantasy as is seen in
Jerry's description of the pornographic playing cards: "What I wanted
to get at is the value difference between pornographic playing cards
when you're older. It's that when you're a kid you use the cards as a
substitute for a real experience, and when you're older you use real
experience as a substitute for the fantasy."[7] What is important here is
that, whether one begins with ideas and moves toward experience or
whether one moves in the opposite direction, a disparity always remains. The recognition of that disparity is the essential content of
Jerry's vision. Whether the process begins with either the idea or the
object, one must inevitably be, in Nancy's terms, a "substitution" for the
other and therefore different in actual identity. That is why the
dialogue between Charlie, Nancy, and their reptilian counterparts
must inevitably fail. No matter that they are joined by a verb; subject
can never be co-incidental with objects, to borrow the terminology of
The Man from *Listening*, no matter how much we may wish it. As with
Seascape, the bulk of Albee's first play comes to be an elaboration of this
vision whose content is the necessary failure of communication.[8] To be
sure, the action of *The Zoo Story* might be described as the process of
translation of Jerry's death fantasy into action, just as the presence of
the sea lizards in *Seascape* is the externalizing of objectification of the
debate between Charlie and Nancy. It is important, however, to emphasize that the phenomenalization of Jerry's fantasy is brought about
through language and that Peter is, significantly enough, a publisher
by profession. Indeed, the process is overtly linguistic. It is the ongoing
process of definition. The play reaches its climax over the argument as
to whether or not Peter is a "vegetable" (pp. 52 ff). In the linguistic
bargaining which takes place, Peter is called upon to take action in
order to deny the validity of the name which has been applied to him.

When in the final twist, Peter proves himself not to be a "vegetable" but rather an "animal," society, at large, is thereby defined as a "zoo," and it is this secret definition, a linguistic riddle of identity, that is the mystery which is at the heart of the play.[9] The play as a whole might, then, well be taken as a type of extended definition. This idea of drama as linguistic process is likewise clearly seen in the playwright's *Counting the Ways*, which serves as little more than an extended definition of love. Remembering that Albee has throughout his career insisted that his writing begins with the creation of characters and then progresses to placing those characters in particular situations,[10] the playwright's work, as has just been seen in *The Zoo Story*, may be seen as unfolding revelations of character and identity. Keeping in mind Elizabeth's pronouncement in *The Lady from Dubuque:* "In the outskirts of Dubuque... I learned — though I doubt I knew I was learning it — that all of the values were relative save one... "Who am I?" All the rest is semantics — liberty, dignity, possession,"[11] those exercises seem to be essentially semantic in nature.

While this preoccupation with the process of definition is not always as center stage as it is in *Counting the Ways*, it is without exception present in Albee's work. Whether in the more naturalistic dialogue of *Virginia Woolf* or in the seeming collection of non-sequiturs of *Listening*, a major topic of conversation — and admittedly there is a great deal more of talking than of action in Albee's plays — is language and, in particular, semantics. In its most absurdist form, this preoccupation is present in the wonderfully comic tale of the confrontation between Mommy and Mrs. Barker over the color of their hats in *The American Dream*, a work which Albee has described as a play about failed communication.[12] The same play also contains such semantic considerations as the difference between a "house" and an "apartment" or between an "enema bag" and an "enema bottle" as well as a wealth of word plays on such words as "badger" and "bumble/bundle." Each of Albee's plays has a host of similar verbal offerings. *Seascape*, because it deals so directly with the problem of language, again provides an excellent example of the relativity of definition through its comic debate between Charlie and Leslie, the male lizard, over the proper name for the front arm/leg.[13] In a semantic exercise which is much in keeping with the debate over the color of Mommy's hat, Charlie begins,

> Charlie: When we meet we...take each other's hands, or whatever, and we...touch....

Nancy: ... Let's greet each other properly, all right? *(Extends her hand again.)* I give you my hand, and you give me your... what *is* that? What is that called?

Leslie: What?

Nancy: *(Indicating Leslie's right arm.)* That there.

Leslie: It's called a leg, of course.

Nancy: Oh. Well, we call this an arm.

Leslie: You have four arms, I see.

Charlie: No; she has two arms. *(Tiny pause.)* And two legs.

Sarah: *(Moves closer to examine Nancy with Leslie.)* And which are the legs?

Nancy: These here. And these are the arms.

Leslie: *(A little on his guard.)* Why do you differentiate?

Nancy: Why do we differentiate, Charlie?

Charlie: *(Quietly hysterical.)* Because they're the ones with the hands on the ends of them.

Nancy: *(To Leslie.)* Yes.

Sarah: *(As Leslie glances suspiciously at Charlie.)* Go on , Leslie; do what Nancy wants you to do. *(To Nancy.)* What is it called?

Nancy: Shaking hands.

Charlie: Or legs (pp. 68–70).

This verbal bartering continues until the inevitable result is achieved. The sea lizard, in a fashion highly reminiscent of Peter's anger at being called a "vegetable," takes umbrage at being termed a "fish." It would seem, then, that the major thrust of *Seascape* may be summed up in Leslie's annoyed response to Charlie's and Nancy's inability to define the human concepts of love and emotion: "We may, or we may not, but we'll never know unless you define your terms. Honestly, the imprecision! You're so thoughtless!" (p. 87). For his part, Charlie at a subsequent moment retorts in kind as he demands of Nancy, "What *standards* are you using? How would *you* know?" (p. 93). The point of these interchanges is that the existential situation of man is that he must, by the nature of his being, attempt to define his terms and standards, although he is also, by nature, incapable of doing so. Given the playwright's interest in Japanese *Noh* drama as well as Charlie's use of the Rinzai Zen Koan, "What is the sound of one hand clapping?" (p. 60), it would appear that Albee's concept of language is essentially Zen in nature.[14] That is, language as a temporal creation is rooted in the phenomenal while the ideas which it attempts to convey find their source in the ontological. The result of this paradox is that definitions are futile attempts to cast the infinite in the garb of the finite and are of necessity doomed to failure. Such exercises ultimately obscure more than they reveal because of a mistaken notion of their completeness and an ill-placed faith in their ability to capture completely the essence of the subject being defined. Hence, all of the semantic debates, whether over the proper names of colors or anatomical features, are always unresolvable because, by presenting only partial or relative truths, language is a means by which one may, in the playwright's own words, go to "great lengths to avoid communication.... Talk in order not to have to listen."[15]

In all of the naming contests which occur throughout his plays, what exists is for the most part a series of futile semantic debates in which each side insists on judging and defining according to its own perceptive standards. As George wryly tells Nick in *Virginia Woolf,* "Every definition has its boundaries, eh?"[16] That definitions are thus implicitly faulty is seen in Oscar's use of the qualifier "as definitions go" (p. 83) in *The Lady from Dubuque.* To be sure, the implicit doubt of the validity of definitions is the key to the play as a whole. After all, the turning point of the play is the miraculous appearance of Elizabeth, the woman who claims to be Jo's mother. In its abruptness, the appearance of Oscar and Elizabeth is much like that of Leslie and Sarah, the sea lizards. Furthermore, as with the reptiles, their appearance seems to be an objectification of what has previously been presented only in the abstract, for the audience has already been given an indirect description of Jo's mother. The dramatic tension comes from the fact that Elizabeth, in the words of Lucinda, is simply "not what [she] imagined" (p. 99) and is completely unknown to Sam, Jo's husband. In other words, the objectification, as with the symbolic acts of both language and drama, conforms to neither the expected nor the known. The play, like so many others by Albee, ends with the audience left in doubt about the meaning of its title. If Elizabeth is aptly described by the title/name "The Lady from Dubuque," then she is, in fact, not Jo's mother since the latter lives in New Jersey (p. 19). The situation is much like that of *Tiny Alice* where the audience must decide whether to apply the name of the play to the visible onstage character or the offstage abstraction. In each case, the title is a name and as such a definition which is part of each and applies fully to neither with the result that the audience is left with the dilemma of how and when to apply the titular definition.

Albee's insistence on the relativity of words seems to rely heavily on the standard linguistic assertion that each speech act derives its meaning from three sources: the meaning of the word in the mind of the speaker, the meaning of the word in the mind of the listener, and, most importantly, the generally accepted meaning of the word in the speech community of which both speaker and listener are members.[17] As has already been seen, Albee's plays can be viewed as his examinations of these complex relationships. The plays regularly take members from different speech communities, dimensions, worlds, or societies and present their attempts at forging or working out a new, common vocabulary. Even when speakers come from the same speech communities, they of necessity spend most of their time attempting to explain their private meanings. However, the lack of a common language can also be fostered in order to create an impassable gulf between characters. YAM in *FAM and YAM: An Imaginary Interview* reassures FAM in regard to a certain critic by saying, "... but after all, you and a man like that just don't talk the same language."[18] Language is thus used both to include and exclude. YAM uses language to establish a communal bond between himself and FAM and at the same time to separate FAM from the community of critics.

The same linguistic exclusion is readily apparent in *Virginia Woolf.* When asked if he and Martha have any children, George replies to Nick, "That's for me to know and you to find out" (p. 39). It is "finding out" or the solving of the riddle that is, within the play, the process of definition. It is only when Nick discovers that the child whom he assumed to be real is, in fact, the product of his hosts' imaginations that even a rudimentary understanding of the dialogue can begin. It is the final revelation that assumed fact is, in reality, fiction which gives all of the previous language its meaning. Before this final revelation, Martha has already berated Nick for his limited understanding:

> You always deal in appearances? ... you don't see anything, do you?
> You see everything but the goddamn mind; you see all the little specks
> and crap, but you don't see what goes on, do you? (pp. 190, 192).

Throughout the play, Nick deals only in the concrete while George and Martha speak the language of abstraction. True communication between Nick and his hosts is impossible, so despite the fact that Nick tells George, "I'll play the charades like you've got 'em set up. . . . I'll play in your language.... I'll be what you say I am" (p. 150), Nick is doomed to failure not merely because he is not as skillful as George at word play but because he has no understanding of either the vocabulary or the rules by which the linguistic game is played, for as George makes clear at the end of the play, the rules are definite and absolute, and there is a penalty to be exacted for their violation.

Despite the fact that it is their immediate presence which acts as the catalyst for the "fun and games" which are acted out before them, Nick and Honey are, in essence, passive observers. When they enter the action at all, they serve solely as the objects of manipulation, despite any illusions which they may have to the contrary. For the most part, they are mere sounding boards, a convenient direction in which to aim speeches made about subjects in a *patois* which is both unknown and unintelligible at the outset of the play. It is little wonder, then, that there is no real communication between the two couples in the course of the night's action. George and Martha have, between themselves, all of the private, mutually exclusive meanings which they assign to events in their lives as well as a mutually agreed upon vocabulary and an enforceable set of rules for its implementation. This is the source of their togetherness, their comic unity. In contrast, there exists no such bond between either George or Martha and either of their guests. When Nick attempts to converse with George, it is as though the two were attempting to converse in two mutually exclusive tongues without the aid of an interpreter. While George is aware of this fact, Nick is not, and George refuses to explain or to translate. In their linguistic exclusion from the conversations between George and Martha, Nick and Honey are, themselves, models or metaphors for the members of the audience, objectified and placed on stage. Like Nick and Honey, the members of the audience, although the "cause" or occasion of the night's performance, are placed in the positions of passive eavesdroppers to the verbal antics of their hosts. The process of the play is for the audience, as well as for the younger couple on stage, the gradual understanding of those antics and games and hence inclusion into the speech community founded by George and Martha. The play, then, is a linguistic exercise, a teaching of language or at least a forging of a common language founded on an initial act of exclusion and followed by an initiation or movement toward inclusion. The comic unity of the play, and Albee has from the outset stoutly maintained that *Virginia Woolf* is a comedy,[19] is its movement from perceived disunity of George's and Martha's seeming non-sequiturs and highly eccentric speech to a perception of the unity or coherence of their speeches as we learn the semantic and lexical rules of their private tongue. This change in perception takes place when the audience ceases to be excluded from and instead becomes a part of the speech community of George and Martha. And it is important to note that this change is a change in the perception of the reality, not in the reality itself. George was, despite appearances, making "sense" all along. That is, the solving of the riddle, the catharsis, the "finding out" as George puts it, is a linguistic and phenomenal rather than an ontological matter. This is, in the last analysis, the same comic action that was the essential structure of Albee's first play, where the solving of the riddle is the passive observer's ultimate recognition that Jerry's seeming nonsequiturs concerning "the zoo" are not unintelligible ravings. Jerry's comments to Peter, like those of George to Nick, make sense and are in fact seen as truthful as soon as one understands the language in which those "ravings" are cast.

Language, then, can serve as a bridge or medium between speaker and listener but only when both parties are fully aware of its rules and nature. When either half of the equation is missing, the result from the linguist's point of view is not really true language. The point is made by Charlie who in *Seascape* tells Nancy that "parrots don't talk; parrots imitate" (p. 66). Here the linguistic principle that thought must precede the speech act is championed.[20] The parrot does not talk because it does not think. It has no awareness of the fact that its utterances comprise human words, and most important of all, it has no understanding of their meanings, either public or private. In this sense, the parrot is like Nick in *Virginia Woolf* or Sam in *The Lady from Dubuque* who both find themselves unwilling and even unconscious participants in a repartee in which they know neither the rules nor the vocabulary. Albee's interest in the epistemological basis of speech is most clearly seen in a brief interchange from *Listening:*

The Girl:	You don't *listen.*
The Woman:	*(As if the Man were not there.)* Well, that may *be.*
The Girl:	Pay attention, rather, is what you don't do. Listen: oh, yes; carefully, to…oh, the sound an idea makes…
The Woman:	…a *thought.*
The Girl:	No; an idea.
The Woman:	As it does what?
The Girl:	*(Thinks about that for a split second.)* Mmmmmm … as the chemical thing happens, and then the electric

thing, and then the muscle; *that* progression. The response — that almost reflex thing, the movement, when an idea happens. *(A strange little smile.)* That *is* the way the brain works, is it not? The way it functions? Chemical, then electric, then muscle? *(The woman does an "et violâ!" gesture.)*

The Man: *(Quiet awe.)* Where does it come from?

The Woman: What?

The Man: The ... all that. Where does it come from?

The Woman: I haven't found out. It all begins right there: she says, "You don't listen." Every time, she says: "You don't listen."

The Man: To what!? You don't listen to what!?

The Woman: *(Sotto voce.)* I don't *know* what I don't listen to.

The Man: *(Accusatory.)* Yes, and do you care?

The Woman: *(So reasonable.)* I DON'T *know.*

The Man: *(Snorting.)* Of course not!

The Woman: *(Quite brusque.)* Defend the overdog once in a while, will you!? At least what you *think* it is. How do you know who's what!?

The Man: I don't!

The Woman: All right!

The Man: (Shrugs; throws it away.) Get behind that sentence, that's all you have to do. Find out what precedes (pp. 73–75).

The passage touches upon all the elements necessary for true linguistic communication as it follows the stages of the unconscious genesis of an idea to its establishment in the consciousness of the speaker to its final articulation and reception by a listener. As the title of the play suggests, the final stage is as important as the first. One must, to quote The Girl, not merely listen but also pay attention. A listener, then, is as important to language as a speaker; without a true listener who pays attention, language must out of necessity fail. As Albee has, himself, pointed out in several interviews, Mommy can tell Mrs. Barker, in *The American Dream* to take off her dress rather than her coat because no one in the room is paying any attention to what anyone else is saying.[21] That is why the play is, according to its author, a play about the failure of communication. Significantly, the need for true communication is so great that

its failure can result in madness. An important part of the "madness" of
The Girl in *Listening* is her resentment over the fact that The Woman
really doesn't "Listen." Similarly, Julian, in *Tiny Alice,* equates his own
descent into madness with a loss of the ability to hear and comprehend
language: "The periods of hallucination would be announced by a
ringing in the ears, which produced, or was accompanied by, a loss of
hearing. I would hear people's voices from a great distance and
through the roaring of...surf. And my body would feel light, and not
mine, and I would float, not glide."[22]

If speaker and listener are essential to the linguistic process,
then one must ask what is the nature of the operation which takes place
between the two. To borrow a phrase from The Man in *Listening,* each
attempts to "get behind" (that is, understand the generating idea) the
sentence or public pronouncement between them. Without the kind of
intuition which Nancy claims in regard to understanding what is in
Charlie's "gut," one must of necessity rely on indirect means such as
symbols or words which are by nature finite compromises for infinite
complexities. An example of the kind of linguistic bartering that is
necessary although futile is found in the description of the wrapped
lunch in *The American Dream:*

Mommy: ... And every day, when I went to school, Grandma used
to wrap a box for me, and I used to take it with me to
school; and when it was lunchtime, all the little boys and
girls used to take out their boxes of lunch, and they
weren't wrapped nicely at all, and they used to open them
and eat their chicken legs and chocolate cakes; and I used
to say, 'Oh, look at my lovely lunch box; it's so nicely
wrapped it would break my heart to open it.' And so, I
wouldn't open it.

Daddy: Because it was empty.

Mommy: Oh no. Grandma always filled it up, because she never ate
the dinner she cooked the evening before; she gave me all
her food for my lunch box the next day. After school, I'd
take the box back to Grandma, and she'd open it and eat
the chicken legs and chocolate cake that was inside.
Grandma used to say, 'I love day-old cake.' That's where
the expression day-old cake came from. Grandma always
ate everything a day late. I used to eat all the other little
boys' and girls' food at school, because they thought my
lunch box was empty, and that's why I wouldn't open it.
They thought I suffered from the sin of pride,and since
that made them better than me, they were very generous.[23]

The point here is that, while there is a seeming common understanding concerning the external appearance of the box, each person believed it to contain something different. In the same fashion, words which seem clear and apparent frequently have individual and sometimes antithetical, private meanings to the characters who use them within the context of the play. Thus, when Grandma in *The American Dream* presents the mysterious boxes around which everyone must negotiate, those boxes are in essence words, and, indeed, Grandma's most consistent complaint throughout the play concerns the way in which everyone speaks to the elderly. Words, then, are to Albee types of decorated boxes sometimes containing wonderful surprises as in the comic debates between Charlie and Leslie, or they can serve as virtual Pandora's boxes as they do in the cases of George and Martha. As FAM says in his interview with YAM, "Words; words…They're such a pleasure" (p. 88), and as George notes, "Martha's a devil with language: she really is" (p. 21).

As the case with George and Martha might suggest, the field of semantics is the arena in which the tug of war between reality and fantasy ultimately takes place. Nowhere is this made clearer than in *Tiny Alice*. In that play, many of Albee's concerns with the symbolic nature of language find their expression in the semantic debate over the curious relationship between the house in which Alice resides and the model which it contains. The house, it seems, was originally constructed in England and then disassembled and rebuilt in its present location. The house, therefore, is not by definition an "original" but is, rather, a "replica." Although built of the materials of the original, the replica can no more be the original than a word can be identical to the mental image which it signifies. The replica once again presents the playwright's preoccupation with the translation of ideas, persons, and objects. Translation, however, in these terms implies an absolute alteration of the item translated, for it implies a definite and distinct change from one location or state of being to another. In the midst of the replica stands a "model"—the proportionately correct although scaled down symbol which is derivative, though wholly separate from the original. It should, however, be noted that the model is subject to the vicissitudes which affect the replica and not *vice versa*. This is seen in the fact that while the fire is first noted in the chapel of the model it is, in fact, put out in the chapel of the replica. As in the case of the fire in the chapel, one learns about the house, the replica, by studying the model. If the model is to be exact, it must contain a model, which, in turn, must contain a model. The process must go on *ad infinitum*. The infinite nature of the series of reflective models required to establish the model as an exact duplicate of the replica presents an example of Xeno's paradox concerning the tortoise and the hare. Just as the hare can never in theory overtake the tortoise, so the model can never reach its goal of reduplicating either the replica or the original.[24]

To understand the complex relationship which Albee is suggesting here, it is necessary to turn to a similar set of relationships in the later play, *Listening*, as The Girl describes the mysterious "blue cardboard":

> Yes. Most cardboard is grey...or brown, heavier. But blue cardboard is...unusual. That would be enough, but if you see blue cardboard, tile blue, love it, want...it, and have it...then it's special. But—don't interrupt me! — Well, if you want more value from it, from the experience, and take *grey* cardboard, mix your colors and paint it, carefully, blue, to the edges, smooth, then it's not *any* blue cardboard but very special: grey cardboard taken and made blue, self-made, self-made blue—better than grey, better than the other blue, because it's self-done. Very valuable, and even looking at it is a theft; touching it, even to take it to a window to see the smooth lovely color, all blue, is a theft. Even the knowledge of it is a theft...of sorts (pp. 99–91).

The blue is the Ideal. It is not only exclusive but practically unattainable. It is the "original" in that it is an intangible, unknowable form, in the Platonic sense. The grey is the common experience or phenomenon. What is of interest here in the artifice of the cardboard painted blue, for like a word or a play it stands mid-way between an action and the idea of that action, taking its identity from both but identical to neither. The artifice is just that; it is an artifice. It is a conscious creation. It is, however, as a result of the hands of the craftsman, no longer grey and yet not quite identical to the object, for it is neither purely an emanation, in the Neo-Platonic sense, nor is it uncreate or original.

However, if both the cardboard made blue as well as the model of the replica are merely finite, imperfect imitations, one must question the very act of resorting to such forms if they, like words, must inevitably fall short of what they attempt to portray or describe. While both the discussions of the model in *Tiny Alice* and the cardboard in *Listening* present the limitations of language as a mediating instrument between the abstract and the concrete, both simultaneously present the argument for the necessity of the linguistic medium, despite its imperfect status. In both cases, the model and the artifice are the only means by which the Abstraction and its relationship to the concrete may be observed and known. Ironically, the very imperfections of language may be said to be the source of its attraction for Albee since its failure to capture completely the Abstract, as it is termed in *Tiny Alice,* is what renders the Abstract comprehensible to the human intellect. Language, as the "glorious imperfect," allows the imperfect to know glory if not perfection.

As the meeting ground of the abstract and the concrete, language serves to help man understand the nature of each. Without that help, man is placed in the dilemma, so common in the plays of Albee, of not being able to distinguish between illusion and reality. This problem of illusion and reality is the exact source of Julian's dilemma in *Tiny Alice.* Such confusion is seen in Julian's remarkable description of an hallucinatory sexual encounter (pp. 61–65). Significantly, Miss Alice responds to Julian's account of his sexual/ecstatic experience with a fellow inmate by asking, "Is the memory of something having happened the same as it having happened?" (p. 65). Her question as to the actual relationship between the real and the imaginary remains the problem with which Julian must grapple throughout the rest of the play, and, in fact, it is central to incidents in the lives of the characters in several other plays as well, for the hallucinatory nature of sexual union is a recurring theme in the works of Albee. The theme is made manifest in *The Zoo Story* in Jerry's description of his relationship with his landlady:

> ... and somewhere, somewhere in the back of that pea-sized brain of hers, an organ developed just enough to let her eat, drink, and emit, she has some foul parody of sexual desire. And I, Peter, am the object of her sweaty lust.
>
> But I have found a way to keep her off. When she talks to me, when she presses herself to my body and mumbles about her room and how I should come there, I merely say: but, Love; wasn't yesterday enough for you, and the day before? Then she puzzles, she makes slits of her tiny eyes, she sways a little, and then, Peter...and it is at this moment that I think I might be doing some good in that tormented house ... a simple-minded smile begins to form on her unthinkable face, and she giggles and groans as she thinks about yesterday and the day before; as she believes and relives what never happened ... (pp. 33–34).

For the landlady, one may indeed say that memory is the equivalent of event. Jerry's obvious distaste over the incident shows that he, like

Julian, is as deeply affected by another's fantasy as if the actual events
had taken place. The same problem arises in *Virginia Woolf* where it is
not the sexual act that is fantasized but rather the product of that act,
the imaginary son. In all of these cases, the best evidence points to the
unreality of the events described, and yet in each case, the hallucination
of the action produces the same effects as the actual event. Hallucination, then, provides a middle ground between idea and event for those
who find the Ideal unattainable and the present unbearable. In *Virginia Woolf*, George makes a similar observation when he notes,

> It's very simple. ... When people can't abide things as they are, when
> they can't abide the present, they do one of two things...either they...
> either they turn to a contemplation of the past, as I have done, or they
> set about to...alter the future (p. 178).

Julian confirms the value of such mediation when he concludes his
description of his hallucinatory encounter by noting,

> I was persuaded, eventually, that perhaps I was...over-concerned by
> hallucination; that some was inevitable, and a portion of that—even
> desirable (p. 64).

In all three instances, Albee relies on the sexual metaphor for this
commingling of illusion and reality, a metaphor commonly found in
the writings of the mystics in their attempts to describe mystical union.
Julian's confusion, here as well as throughout his life, is the direct result
of his rejection of a middle ground, of the possible union of the
Absolute and the relative which is achieved in both the made-over
cardboard and the model of the replica. In the third act of the play, the
other characters attempt to apprise him of this very folly:

Lawyer: *(Sarcasm is gone; all is gone, save fact.)* Dear Julian; we all
           serve, do we not? Each of us his own priesthood; public-
           ly, some, others ... within only; but we all do — what's-
           his-name's special trumpet, or clear lonely bell. Predes-
           tination, fate, the will of God, accident.... All swirled up
           in it, no matter what the name. And being man, we have
           invented choice, and have, indeed, gone further, and
           have catalogued the underpinnings of choice. But we do
           not know. Anything. End prologue.

Miss Alice: Tell him.

Lawyer:	No Matter. We are leaving you now, Julian; agents, every one of us — going. We are leaving you … to your accomplishment: your marriage, your wife, your…special priesthood.
Julian:	*(Apprehension and great suspicion.)* I … don't know what you're talking about.
Lawyer:	*(Unperturbed.)* What is so amazing is the … coming together … of disparates … left-fielding, out of the most unlikely. Who would have thought, Julian? Who would have thought? You have brought us to the end of our service here. We go on; you stay.
Butler:	May I begin to cover?
Miss Alice:	Not Yet. *(Kindly)* Do you understand, Julian?
Julian:	*(Barely in control.)* Of course not!
Miss Alice:	Julian, I have tried to be…*her*. No; I have tried to be… what I thought she might, what might make you happy, what you might use, as a … what?
Butler:	*Play* God; go on.
Miss Alice:	We must…represent, draw pictures, reduce or enlarge to…to what we can understand.
Julian:	*(Sad, mild.)* But I have fought against it … all my life. When they said, 'Bring the wonders down to me, closer; I cannot see them, touch; nor can I believe.' I have fought against it…all my life.
Butler:	*(To Miss Alice; softly.)* You see? No good.
Miss Alice:	*(Shrugs.)* I have done what I can do with it.
Julian:	All my life. In and out of…confinement, fought against the symbol.
Miss Alice:	Then you should be happy now.
Cardinal:	Julian, it has been our desire always to serve; your sense of mission…
Lawyer:	We are surrogates; *our* task is done now.
Miss Alice:	Stay with her.
Julian:	*(Horror behind it; disbelieving.)* Stay…with…her?
Miss Alice:	Stay with her. Accept it.
Lawyer:	*(At the model.)* Her rooms are lighted. It is warm, there is enough.
Miss Alice:	Be content with it. Stay with her.
Julian:	*(Refusing to accept what he is hearing.)* Miss Alice…I have married *you*.

Miss Alice:	*(Kind, still.)* No, Julian; you have married *her*...through me.
Julian:	*(Pointing to the model.)* There is nothing there! We are *here!* There is no one *there!*
Lawyer:	*She* is there...we believe.
Julian:	*(To Miss Alice.)* I have been with *you!*
Miss Alice:	*(Not explaining; sort of dreamy.)* You have felt her warmth through me, touched her lips through my lips, held her hands, through mine, my breasts, hers, lain on her bed, through mine, wrapped yourself in her wings, your hands on the small of her back, your mouth on her hair, the voice in your ear, hers not mine, all hers; her. You are hers.
Cardinal:	Accept.
Butler:	Accept.
Lawyer:	Accept (pp. 160–163).

This dialogue presents the beginning of Julian's awe-filled recognition of the price exacted by his rejection of symbols, for Alice herself admits that she is merely a symbol, an imperfect attempt to represent the abstract. Everyone is, as the lawyer notes, an "agent," a representative of a thing, rather than the thing itself. The wedding itself is a symbol of mediation or union. Julian as a *lay brother* is himself an apt symbol of the very kind of mediation which he has spent his life trying to reject. Yet Julian's rejection of such mediation has been his distinguishing characteristic throughout the play. The true extent of Julian's dualistic vision, as well as its dire consequences, is seen in his own account of the cause of his madness:

Julian:	Oh... *(Pause.)* I...I lost my faith. *(Pause.)* In God.
Butler:	Ah. *(Then a questioning look.)*
Julian:	Is there more?
Butler:	*Is* there more?
Julian:	Well, nothing...of matter. I...declined. I...shriveled into myself; a glass dome...descended, and it seemed I was out of reach, unreachable, finally unreaching, in this...paralysis, of sorts. I...put myself in a mental home.
Butler:	*(Curiously noncommittal.)* Ah.

Julian: I could not reconcile myself to the chasm between the nature of God and the use to which man put ... God.

Butler: Between your God and others', your view and theirs.

Julian: I said what I intended: *(Weighs the opposites in each hand.)* It is God the mover, not God the puppet; God the creator, not the God created by man.

Butler: *(Almost pitying.)* Six years in the loony bin of semantics?

Julian: *(Slightly flustered, heat.)* It is not semantics! Men create a false God in their own image, it is easier for them! ... It is not ... (pp. 43–44).

The passage is the key to Julian's thinking as it clearly shows that to Julian the difference between the First Cause and its emanations, between an object and the perception of that object, is both real and irreconcilable. Furthermore, the movement is essentially Neo-Platonic since the contrasting movement from experience to abstraction, namely man's creation of God, is rejected out of hand. Because the distinction is real, it is not in Julian's eyes "semantic," that is, without substance. Julian then is rejecting what he believes to be the relative in favor of the Absolute.

In order to understand more fully the exact nature of Julian's rejection of the label "semantic" to describe the difference between idea and emanation, it is necessary to consider a case in which he feels that the term is appropriate:

Butler: *(To Julian, pointing first to the model, then to the room.)* Do you mean the model ... or the replica?

Julian: I mean the ... I mean ... what we are in.

Butler: *Ah*-ha. And which is that?

Julian: That we are in?

Butler: Yes.

Lawyer: *(To Julian.)* You are clearly not a Jesuit. *(Turning.)* Butler, you've put him in a clumsy trap.

Butler: *(Shrugging.)* I'm only a servant.

Lawyer: *(To Julian, too sweetly.)* You needn't accept his alternative ... that since we are clearly not in a model we must be in a replica.

Butler: *(Vaguely annoyed.)* Why must he not accept that?

Miss Alice: Yes. Why not?

Lawyer:	I said he did not *need* to accept the alternative. I did not say it was not valid.
Julian:	*(Cheerfully.)* I will not accept it; the problem is only semantic (pp. 85–86).

To Julian the relationship between the model and the replica, as opposed to the relationship between God and the world, is semantic. The difference between idea and event is absolute; the differences between the various emanations of that idea are not. Language is, to Julian, part of the phenomenal. It is not, like the grey cardboard painted blue, a bridge from one realm to the other, for Julian would reject the artifice of the cardboard as an Aristotelian movement from the concrete to the abstract, since that is the movement which Julian wishes to avoid. Julian's reaction is to resolve the tension of that duality not by transcendence of the oppositions or by accepting their existence and arranging them hierarchically but rather through a complete dismissal of the phenomenal. Because Julian sees the use of symbols of a lessening of the Abstract, he rejects it out of hand. The Lawyer replies,

> I have learned...Brother Julian...never to confuse the representative of a... thing with the thing itself (p. 39).

In other words, the corruption of the Cardinal who is the subject of the dialogue in no way diminishes the God for which he stands. The manipulation of the symbol does not affect the idea which it represents. Again, that is why the fire, although first seen in the model, must be extinguished in the replica. The destruction of the chapel must be reflected in the model for its purpose is to reflect the replica as it is, not as it was. The fire, of course, has no effect on the original which exits only in memory and is no longer affected by events in the real world. Thus, Julian's fear that symbols constitute a lessening of the Abstract is proven to be groundless.

The lawyer, with the butler acting out the role of Julian, demonstrates the folly of the confusion under which Julian suffers:

Lawyer:	But *shall* we tell him the whole thing? The Cardinal? What is happening?
Butler:	How much can he take?
Lawyer:	He is a man of God, however much he simplifies, however much he worships the symbol and not the substance.

Butler: Like everyone.

Lawyer: Like most.

Butler: Julian can't stand that; he told me so: men make God in their own image, he said. Those six years I told you about.

Lawyer: Yes. When he went into an asylum. YES.

Butler: It was — because he could not stand it, wasn't it? The use men put God to.

Lawyer: It's perfect; wonderful.

Butler: Could not reconcile.

Lawyer: No.

Butler: God as older brother, scout leader, couldn't take that.

Lawyer: And still not reconciled.

Butler: Has pardoned men, I think. Is walking on the edge of an abyss, but is balancing. Can be pushed ... over, back to the asylums.

Lawyer: Or over...to the Truth. *(Addressing Julian, as if he were there; some thunder in the voice.)* God, Julian? Yes? God? *Whose* God? Have you pardoned men their blasphemy, Julian? Have you forgiven them?

Butler: *(Quiet echoing answers; being Julian.)* No, I have not, have not really; have *let* them, but cannot accept.

Lawyer: Have not forgiven. No Julian. Could you ever?

Butler: *(Ibid.)* It is their comfort, my agony.

Lawyer: Soft God? The servant? Gingerbread God with the raisin eyes?

Butler: *(Ibid.)* I cannot accept it.

Lawyer: Then don't accept it, Julian.

Butler: But there is *some*thing. There is a *true* God.

Lawyer: There is an abstraction, Julian, but it cannot be understood. You cannot worship it.

Butler: *(Ibid.)* There is more.

Lawyer: There is Alice, Julian. That can be understood. Only the mouse in the model. Just that.

Butler: *(Ibid.)* There must be more.

Lawyer: The mouse. Believe it. Don't personify this abstraction, Julian, limit it, demean it. Only the mouse, the toy. And that does not exist...but is all that can be worshipped....Cut off from it, Julian, ease yourself, ease off. No trouble now; accept it.

Butler: *(Talking to Julian now.)* Accept it, Julian; ease off. Worship
           it...
Lawyer: Accept it (pp. 105–107).

This play within a play not only makes its point in and about the
abstract but goes on to provide its corroboration in fact since the butler,
named Butler in another convenient merging of idea and actuality, by
acting the role of Julian has not affected Julian in any real sense. The
problem, as the Lawyer sets it forth, is that the Abstract is, as Julian
claims, unknowable and ineffable. Julian is correct to that extent, and
yet like everyone else Julian has continued to pursue that unattainable
knowledge. What sets Julian apart is his refusal to accept the necessary
compromise or mediation which such a paradox demands. By refusing
to accept mediation which others accept, Julian has only placed the
Abstract farther beyond his reach. By rejecting symbols, Julian is
abandoning all that may be known of the Absolute on the non-mystical,
conscious level. Julian has ultimately deceived himself into believing
that he has, in fact, completely rejected the mediation of language and
symbol in his striving to experience the divine. Yet to speak and think of
the Absolute as Julian does or, for that matter, even to resort to the term
"Absolute" is indeed a denial of the recognition of its ineffability.

It is the recognition of this self-deception which comprises the
bulk of Julian's final soliloquy. Deserted and dying at the play's conclusion, Julian realizes that in marrying Miss Alice he has, as the lawyer
said, unknowingly accepted the symbol as a reality, for without the
symbol "THE ABSTRACTION" is too terrible to behold. Julian's final
words, as if in answer to the earlier pleas of both the lawyer and the
butler are, "I accept thee, Alice, for thou art come to me. God, Alice...I
accept thy will" (p. 189). The ultimate proclamation of Julian's folly,
however, comes in Julian's realization that he is facing death. Julian has
imagined Death, not dying. He knows life, the phenomenal, and has
imagined Death, the ontological, but he has never given any thought to
dying, the act of translation, the middle ground between the two.

Significantly, in the act of dying Julian assumes the attitude of
the crucified Christ, another mediator between the Abstract and the
concrete. Death is the ineffable state. Dying, however, may be known
and described. In the last analysis, Julian is of a kind with Albee's many
other characters such as Peter and Nick who are lost in the midst of
verbal exchanges of which they had no understanding. However, while
Julian's dilemma is ultimately linguistic in nature, he is not merely a

man who cannot understand the language in which the oblique discussions of the mysterious Alice are couched. He is, until the final lines of the play, a man who will not understand because he rejects language and symbol as an unnecessary, even unacceptable compromise. He is not able to live comfortably in a world where all Truth and, therefore, meaning are in George's words, "relative." Yet, it is the very compromise which has been at the thematic and structural centers of Albee's work from its inception, and it is the basis for the playwright's initial reaction to the interviewers' question concerning the place of realism in theatre. As he has noted in several interviews, the ultimate task of the playwright is "to turn fact into truth,"[25] and this is the compromise of both the playwright and the linguist.

Notes

[1]"The Pitfalls of Drama" is a chapter sub-heading in S. I. Hayakawa's *Language in Thought and Action* (New York: Harcourt, Brace, Jovanovich, 1941). Hayakawa discusses the phenomenon of an audience's confusing an actor with the role which he plays as analogous to mistaking a symbol for its referent. The latter confusion will be shown to be an important recurring theme in Albee's works, especially *Tiny Alice*.

[2]"Playwrights Talk on Writing, Number 1: Edward Albee" (Taped Interview), The Dramatic Publishing Company, Chicago, Illinois.

[3]While critics have consistently lavished praise on Albee's use of language and, especially, dialogue, relatively little attention has been paid to the playwright's concept or theory of the linguistic medium. Notable exceptions to this rule are Linda Woods, "Isolation and the Barrier of Language in *The Zoo Story*," *Research Studies* 36 (1968):224–31; Thomas P. Adler, "Art or Craft: Language in the Plays of Edward Albee," in *Planned Wilderness* (Edinburgh, Tx.: Pan American University, 1980), pp. 45–57; Arthur K. Oberg, "Edward Albee: His Language and Imagination," *Prairie Schooner* 40 (1966):139–46; Brian Way, "Albee and the Absurd: *The American Dream* and *The Zoo Story*" in *American Theatre*, Stratford-Upon-Avon Series No. 10, (New York: St. Martin's, 1967), pp. 188–207; and Gerald Weales, "Edward Albee: Don't Make Waves" in *Jumping Off Place: American Drama in the 1960s* (New York: Macmillan, 1969), pp. 24–53.

[4]Edward Albee, *Seascape* (New York: Atheneum, 1975), pp. 34–36. All subsequent page references appear in the text.

[5]Edward Albee, *Counting the Ways and Listening: Two Plays* (New York: Atheneum, 1977), p. 128. All subsequent page references appear in the text.

[6]The theme of the relationship between the Ideal and the Actual or Illusion and Truth has long been recognized as an important theme running through many of Albee's works. See Mary Long, "Interview: Edward Albee," *Mademoiselle* (Au-

gust 1976):230, as well as Robert M. Post, "Cognitive Dissonance in the Plays of Edward Albee," *Quarterly Journal of Speech* 55 (February 1976):54–60; Lawrence Kingsley, "Reality and Illusion: A Continuity of Theme in Albee," *Educational Theatre Journal (ETJ)* 25 (March 1973):71–9; and Robert W. Corrigan, "Engagement/Disengagement in Contemporary Theatre," in *The Theatre in Search of a Fix* (New York: Delacorte, 1973), pp. 278–82.

[7]Edward Albee, *The Zoo Story, The Death of Bessie Smith, The Sandbox: Three Plays Introduced by the Author* (New York: Coward, McCann & Geoghegan, 1960), p. 32. All subsequent page references to these three plays appear in the text.

[8]For treatments of the theme of failed communication, see Woods as well as Thomas E. Porter, "Fun and Games in Suburbia: *Who's Afraid of Virginia Woolf?*" contained in *Myth and Modern American Drama* (Detroit: Wayne State University Press, 1969), pp. 225–47, and Carol A. Sykes, "Albee's Beast Fables: *The Zoo Story* and *A Delicate Balance*," *ETJ* 25 (December 1973):448–55.

[9]The problem of "identity" is another theme which appears in many of Albee's works. See C. W. E. Bigsby, *Confrontation and Commitment: A Study of Contemporary American Drama, 1959–1960* (Kansas City: University of Missouri Press, 1967), pp. 71–92.

[10]For Albee's descriptions of his creative method, see the following interviews: Paul Zindel and Loree Yerby, "Interview: Edward Albee," *Wagner Literary Magazine* No. 3 (1962):1–10; Thomas Lask, "Edward Albee at Ease," *New York Times*, 27 October 1963, Section 2, p. 1; and "Albee: 'I Write to Unclutter My Mind,'" *New York Times*, 26 January 1975, p. 1.

[11]Edward Albee, *The Lady from Dubuque* (New York: Atheneum, 1980), pp. 151–52. All subsequent page references appear in the text.

[12]Charles S. Krohn and Julian N. Wasserman, "An Interview with Edward Albee, 3/18/81." See above, p. 19.

[13]For a clear and concise explanation of the semantic processes involved, see Hayakawa, especially pp. 179–87.

[14]See Diasetz T. Suzuki, *Zen and Japanese Culture* (Princeton: Princeton University Press, 1970), for discussions of Noh Drama (pp. 419–27) and the Zen theory of language (pp. 6–10, 155 ff.).

[15]Krohn and Wasserman. See above, p. 19.

[16]Edward Albee, *Who's Afraid of Virginia Woolf?: A Play* (New York: Atheneum, 1978), p. 40. All further page references appear in the text.

[17]See L. M. Myers, *American English, A Twentieth Century Grammar* (New York: Prentice-Hall, 1952).

[18]Edward Albee, *Fam and Yam: An Imaginary Interview* contained in *The Sandbox, The Death of Bessie Smith (With Fam and Yam)* (New York: New American Library, 1960), p. 80.

[19]See Otis L. Guernsey, "Edward Albee Confronts Broadway, 1966," *Diplomat*, October 1966, pp. 60–63.

[20]See Peter Farb, *Word Play: What Happens When People Talk* (New York: Knopf, 1974) for a discussion of thought and language (pp. 191 ff.) and of the peculiar case of parrots and other imitative birds (pp. 258–9).

[21]Krohn and Wasserman. See above, p. 19.

[22]Edward Albee, *Tiny Alice* (New York: Atheneum, 1965), p. 60. All subsequent page references appear in the text.

[23]Edward Albee, *The American Dream* (New York: Coward, McCann & Geoghegan, 1961), pp. 21–22. All further page references appear in the text.
[24]See Frederick Copleston, S.J., *A History of Philosophy, Volume I: Greece and Rome* (Westminster, Md.: Newman Bookshop, 1946), pp. 56–58.
[25]Krohn and Wasserman. See above, p. 15.

Disturbing Our Sense of Well-Being
The "Uninvited" in *A Delicate Balance*

I N THE FIRST SCENE of the second act of *A Delicate Balance*, Agnes tells Julia about a recently published book: "It is a book to be read and disbelieved, for it disturbs our sense of well-being."[1] Ironically, Agnes' rather terse critical pronouncement might just as aptly be applied to the literary piece in which she herself appears, for by challenging and disturbing the "well-being" of critics and audience alike the play has continued to spark mixed critical response since it was first produced in September 1966. Terence Brown, after acknowledging this mixed reception, paradoxically states that "most of [Albee's] critics, including many of the severest, agree that the Pulitzer Prize-winning *A Delicate Balance* is probably his most mature play."[2] John J. von Szeliski goes even further, asserting that "*A Delicate Balance* is Albee's best play—and that it ranks as a truly major drama."[3] One wonders, then, why this play has met with such unsympathetic criticism, ranging from a review in *The New Republic* where Brustein called the play "a very bad play" to a review in *The Commonweal* in which Wilfrid Sheed criticized the play for being unbelievable.[4] Perhaps it is precisely because the play *does* disturb one's sense of well-being that critics have judged it so harshly, not recognizing that *A Delicate Balance* is intended to point out the fragile nature of that illusion of security by exploring the ill-defined boundaries which separate sanity from madness and by exposing just how delicate those boundaries can be, even in a seemingly calm household like that of Agnes and Tobias.

From the beginning of the play, the subject of Agnes' conversation is incongruous not only with the well-ordered setting in which it takes place but also with Agnes' oddly detached attitude. In the living room of a well-appointed suburban house, most likely in Connecticut, one would expect a conversation about golf scores and the Dow Jones average rather than the wistful musings of Agnes on what it would be like to lose one's mind. She approaches the subject with ethereal high-mindedness, as if a descent into madness were nothing more than a graceful release. Her lyrical description of madness suggests floating upward, a spiritual transcendence: "... some gentle loosening of the moorings sending the balloon adrift — and I think that is the only outweighing thing: adrift: the... becoming a stranger in... the world, quite...involved, for I never see it as violent, only a drifting..." (p. 13).

Despite the fact that Agnes' casual consideration of the prospect of madness at first seems merely a bit of metaphoric whimsy in light of her apparent stability and affluence, one senses an undercurrent of apprehension in the fitful stops and starts, the sudden interjection of the concrete with the disconcerting reference to Agnes' sister Claire, and finally in the confused syntax. Moreover, the last line indicates that such thoughts are not the products of the moment but have been continually entertained many times before. As the play progresses, Agnes' reasons for her preoccupation with madness become more clear, particularly after she reveals her reaction to her son's death. In a rare moment of vulnerability, Agnes speaks of the existential doubts which brought her to the edge of insanity: "It was an unreal time: I thought Tobias was out of love with me—or rather, was tired of it, when Teddy died, as if that had been the string.... Ah, the things I doubted then, that I was loved — that *I* loved, for that matter! — that Teddy had ever lived at all—my mind, you see" (p. 109). The uncertainty and the loss of memory associated here with insanity are an echo of Albee's earlier play *Tiny Alice* in which Julian describes what he has called a nervous breakdown: "And when I was away from myself— never far enough, you know, to... blank, just to... fog over—when I was away from myself I could not sort out my imaginings from what was real."[5]

Significantly, for both Agnes and Julian, madness is portrayed as a confusing and painful loss of identity. For both, it is a frightful wrenching away from the known rather than the graceful slipping away of Agnes' first speech. After Miss Alice asks him, "Are you sure you're not describing what passes for sanity?" (p. 60), Julian gives a speech similar in stops and starts to the one Agnes gives; only Julian's doubts go even further: "But one night... now, there! You see? I said "one night," and I'm not sure, even now, whether or not this thing happened or, if it did not happen, it did or did not happen at noon, or in the morning, much less at night... yet I say night" (p. 61). Miss Alice neatly sums up the problem by asking, "Is the memory of something having happened the same as it having happened?" (p. 64). If such an important connection for the individual's sense of himself and the world as personal memory can so easily fail, then sanity may be more tenuous than one would like to believe. Julian no longer knows whether or not he can trust his own mind, just as Agnes after her son's death could no longer be sure if she loved or if Teddy had even lived. Thus, what seem to be the most basic facts of one's life can come into doubt with even a slight shift in the weight on the balancing board between sanity and madness.

Because Agnes has experienced this uncertainty, she is at the same time both intrigued and frightened by the prospect of madness. In the opening scene, she protects herself from what she fears by describing a descent into madness in ethereal terms. Induced madness is particularly appealing to Agnes because it substitutes control for uncertainty, predictability for spontaneity. By exploring the possibility of insanity in palatable terms, Agnes can feel as if she is gaining some measure of control over that which she fears most. However, despite her attempts to maintain order by redefining liabilities into assets and to prevent the unpredictable through the sheer power of the will, the "uninvited" comes—as if to stay. Despite Agnes' suggestion that she can control events by what she thinks—"And I promise you as well that I shall think good thoughts—healthy ones, positive—and to ward off madness, should it come by—uninvited" (p. 21)—she soon discovers that mental well-being is not a function of the strength or weakness of an individual's will.

Agnes and Tobias, it seems, have been successful up to this point in avoiding the unexpected, largely by insisting on maintaining their control over themselves and their environment. For Agnes and Tobias, life has been a matter of stability and implementing one's will rather than of responding with emotion or flexibility. Nowhere is this more powerfully evident than in Agnes' eloquent speech to Julia: "'To keep in shape.' Have you ever heard the expression? Most people misunderstand it, assume it means alteration, when it does not. Maintenance. When we keep something in shape, we maintain its shape —whether we are proud of that shape, or not, is another matter—we keep *it* from falling apart. We do not attempt the impossible. We maintain. We hold...I shall...keep this family in shape. I shall maintain it, hold it" (p. 88).

Tobias, also, with his motto of "We do what we can" (p. 19), believes in the power of the will to establish order. When that proves to be a failure as the play progresses, Tobias' distress at no longer being able to control events is manifested in his frantic demand that Harry remain: "I DON'T WANT YOU HERE! YOU ASKED?! NO! I DON'T *(loud)* BUT BY CHRIST YOU'RE GOING TO STAY HERE! YOU'VE GOT THE RIGHT! THE RIGHT! DO YOU KNOW THE WORD? THE RIGHT!...AND BY GOD YOU'RE GOING TO TAKE IT! DO YOU HEAR ME?!" (pp. 166–7). Hysterical, Tobias commands Harry to stay, but his orders are merely manifestations of the frustration Tobias feels in not being able to bring order through his commands.

In the course of the play, Tobias must confront the limits of his will along with the limits of friendship and love. Control is the antithesis of spontaneity and healthy love, a lesson that Tobias and Agnes can learn only when they are forced to surrender some of that control, which for both Agnes and Tobias is often manifested in language — especially in definitions. Critics have remarked that the language in this play is pretentious and self-conscious, overlooking the fact that such language intentionally calls attention to itself as a weapon against the "uninvited" and as a protection against the "dark side of reason" (p. 175). To have the proper words in a situation, like having the right glass for one's cognac, is to create stability and maintain order. As von Szeliski notes, "Even in crises, formal conversation rules apply. Talking about Julia, Tobias reports she is in hysterics and Agnes says, 'That is a condition; I inquired about an action.' When Agnes says she will suffer the mantle of the drill sergeant, she is really speaking of the discipline of *talk*."[6]

Conversation is, then, a means of control as well as protection. When Tobias suggests to Agnes that she should apologize to Claire, Agnes parries with a clever linguistic reversal: "Apologize! To her? To Claire? I have spent my adult life apologizing *for* her; I will not double my humiliation by apologizing *to* her" (p. 17). Tobias' response underscores the attention paid to words — "One does not apologize to those for whom one must?" (p. 17) — a retort delightful for its conciseness as well as for its demonstration that he too can play this verbal game. However, while Tobias displays his skill at this repartee, he, much more than Agnes, clearly understands the inherent limitations of language. In spite of his hope that he might help Julia by means of a "serious" talk, Tobias still doubts that such a talk will have any ameliorative effect on his daughter: "If I saw some point to it, I might—if I saw some reason, chance. If I thought, I might...break through to her, and say, 'Julia...,' but then what would I say? 'Julia...' Then, nothing" (p. 42). Agnes replies, "If we do not love someone...never have loved them...." But Tobias reveals a deeper understanding: "No; there can be silence, even having" (p. 42). Tobias understands the mysteries of the ineffable better than Agnes, but perhaps Agnes *needs* the weapon of language more than Tobias does. In Agnes' speech to Claire, she leaves no room for a response, her eloquence protecting her from whatever Claire might say to defend herself or accuse Agnes. In a *tour de force*, Agnes tells Claire:

> If you come to the dinner table unsteady, if when you try to say good evening and weren't the autumn colors lovely today you are nothing but vowels, and *if* one smells the vodka on you from across the room— and *don't* tell me again, *either* of you! that vodka leaves nothing on the breath: if you are expecting it, if you are sadly and wearily expecting it, it does... if these conditions exist... *persist*... if I should scold, it is because I wish I needn't. If I am sharp, it is because I am neither less nor more than human... I apologize for being articulate (p. 23).

Her apology for being articulate could not be more sarcastic since it is her very ability to be articulate which allows her to have the last word; indeed, language is her most powerful weapon against what she perceives as the threatening alliance between Tobias and Claire. Verbal dexterity is Agnes' weapon against what she cannot understand, articulateness her mooring in the world.

In contrast to Agnes' remarkable eloquence, Harry's and Edna's description of what drove them out of their house is marked by confusion and struggle. They search for the words to express the fear so central to the play; that they cannot articulate the feeling of being lost and frightened in their own house is part of the terror. Unlike the fear felt by Agnes, the primal fear experienced by Harry and Edna is ill-defined, and, hence, it is a fear which cannot be controlled by language. Albee thus suggests that man's deepest fears are ineffable, unable to be assuaged by words. This realization, on the parts of the characters, creates an inconsolable sense of isolation, for as Robert Post points out, "Fear is a major fulcrum around which Albee's play is built. The fear is one which the characters realize but it is one which they are unable to define. It seems to be the kind of fear that all mankind has— fear which man realizes but which he cannot communicate to others or to himself."[7]

Agnes' attempt to order the world in such neat fashion is eclipsed by the chaos that arrives uninvited — "the disease". Agnes' eloquence is, after all, no weapon against the dread with which Harry and Edna confront her. Precisely because speech is her weapon, she is less armed against "the disease" when it arrives uninvited. In *Lady From Dubuque,* Sam is in a similar predicament. The wittiest and most articulate character at the beginning of the play, he is the most disturbed by the unexpected guests who come to help his wife through her very real disease. Sam takes longer to see these daemons as anything other than menacing characters, his intuitive sense having been blocked out by his reliance on language. In the face of disease—for Sam, his wife's cancer and for Agnes and Tobias, this mysterious "plague" — words cannot express, let alone dispel, fear. Sounding like children, Harry and Edna try to describe their primeval feeling: "We got...scared...We...were... terrified ... we were scared. It was like being lost: very young again, with the dark, and lost. There was no...thing...to be frightened of, but ... WE WERE FRIGHTENED ... AND THERE WAS NOTHING" (p. 55). The pauses indicate how difficult it is for them to express what they have felt.

Critics have speculated about the source of Harry's and Edna's fear; C.W.E. Bigsby borrows from William James and Leo Tolstoy, saying they are faced with "an irremediable sense of precariousness" and an awareness of the "meaningless absurdity of life."[8] However, for critics to give a name to the fear is to make the same mistake as Agnes and Tobias, to limit with language. Moreover, Harry's and Edna's own words tell us what they are afraid of — "nothing, NOTHING." The nature of this "nothing" becomes crucial to the whole play, serving as it does as a backdrop to the attempts to maintain order. In effect, the "nothing" of which Harry and Edna are so frightened is a Nothing which nonetheless has substance; that is, the Abyss or the Void. Harry and Edna find themselves face to face with the pre-Logos nothingness —the emptiness before the order of language, before identity, before existence. That void is similar to what Agnes experiences when she doubted if Teddy ever existed. For a terrifying moment, Harry and Edna glimpse what the world would be without the meaning created by externally imposed patterns and structures. Because the emptiness which Harry and Edna feel comes from nothing in particular, their fear is even more startling than that of Agnes, whose doubts result from her son's death. Without a particular cause, the disease would seem to have no cure. Circumstance protects no more than does language. Albee deliberately disturbs the balance because, as von Szeliski says, Albee wants us "to deal with our emptiness through first understanding it."[9] Albee changes the patterns to reveal the Nothingness behind those patterns, exposing the connections and constructs which serve as moorings. Speaking for the playwright, Claire ridicules these patterns: "... the rules of the guestbook—be polite. We have our friends and guests for patterns, don't we?—known qualities. The drunks stay drunk; the Catholics go to Mass, the bounders bound. We can't have changes — throws the balance off" (p. 150).

Albee, of course, intends to throw his audience off balance, knowing that only through shifting the patterns can the patterns be revealed. At another point, Agnes says to Claire: "Those are the ground rules." Claire then turns to Tobias with a sad smile, "Tobias? Nothing? Are those the ground rules? Nothing? Too...settled? Too... dried up? Gone?" (p. 39). Although Claire is referring to Tobias' lack of intervention in the ground rules, Albee uses this conversation to refer to the situation he creates where such ground rules no longer apply, where "my room" becomes "our room" which is turn becomes "*the* room." Boundaries change, and limits reveal themselves to be mere functions of a particular situation Albee creates, not Platonic universals true for all cases and all times.

When Harry and Edna, on the basis of their friendship with Agnes and Tobias, move into Julia's room, they feel their relationship supercedes that of Julia who returns "home" after the failure of her fourth marriage. Julia is surprised to find herself "dispossessed." The confusion of the situation is indicated by the personal pronouns in Tobias' remark to Agnes: "I almost went into *my* room...by habit...by mistake, rather, but then I realized that your room is my room because my room is Julia's because Julia's is..." (p. 13). Because the ground rules have changed — friends taking precedence over family — possessive pronouns have virtually lost their meanings; the simple terms of ownership have been called into question. The questions of propriety so easily answered at the beginning of the play with the implied question of "What belongs where?"—the cognac in the glass—have been replaced by the more important but more difficult question of "Who belongs where?"

Claire and Julia discuss the new situation, and Julia says, "But that's my room," to which Claire replies, "It's...the *room*. Happens you were in it. You're a visitor as much as anyone, now." Julia, in turn, answers with a small whine, "But I *know* that room" (p. 99). One must ask, then, if knowledge is a necessary criterion of ownership, just as Alice demanded to know if the memory of an event was the same as its occurrence. Yet within the linguistic debate of *A Delicate Balance,* Julia, like Julian in *Tiny Alice,* seems to be fighting a losing battle. It is little wonder that her frustration becomes unbearable, upset as she is not only by being dispossessed but by losing her grasp on the criteria for possession. To Julia, the orderly world of her parents where logic reigned has become an incomprehensible game of chance. Her place has been usurped, and she does not know how or why this has happened. Edna grandly offers "her" room to Julia when Julia asks her mother for a room in which she can rest. The ground rules have changed with no explanation. Not only has Julia lost her room, but now the terms by which she had assumed it to be hers have been removed as well. In a very real sense, her identity is in question. Is it any wonder, then, that her frustrated response is a hysterical "I want... WHAT IS MINE!" (p. 108)? Agnes answers coolly, "Well, then, my dear, you will have to decide what that is, will you not?" (p. 108). The point here is not that such decisions can ultimately be made with any degree of certainty but, rather, that such decisions are necessary compromises made for the sake of one's mental well being in the face of the infinite.

The crisis of the room thus juxtaposes the rights of friends with the rights of family. Tobias wants to believe in the possibility of unconditional love in friendship and, therefore, wants to overlook Julia's claim to her room in favor of redefining the boundaries of friendship. Because he wants to offer unconditional friendship, out of both duty and his own needs rather than love, Tobias becomes obsessed with the right of Harry and Edna to stay. As Robert M. Post notes, "Even though in reality there is no deep bond between these 'friends,' Tobias insists that the fact that they are labelled as 'friends' gives them the right to live in his house."[10] It is Claire who earlier in the play says that love is not enough, but it is poor Tobias who has to learn what he can and cannot give.

Thus, if the play chronicles the rapid destruction of the sense of well-being among its central characters, it does so by making them aware of the limits or boundaries of human existence: limits of love, limits of language, limits to the control which one has over his own life, limits of self and self-expression. Within the course of the play, all learn that the boundaries of space and friendship and even family are neither fixed nor immutable and are but false stars by which they may only temporarily plot the course of their own lives, for the world of the play is an existential realm in which the accumulated patterns of a lifetime may be lost in an instant.

In the last act, Claire ironically muses, "Just think, Tobias, what would happen if the patterns changed, you wouldn't know where you stood, and the world would be full of strangers; that would never do" (p. 150). The supreme irony here is that Claire speaks as though such a change in patterns were a mere possibility, and a remote one at that, rather than the absolute certainty which such change has proven to be throughout the play. For all intents and purposes, the world is already full of strangers, strangers to each other, to those most intimate, even to themselves. Perhaps it is Edna who sees the truth most clearly: "It's sad to know you've gone through it all, or most of it, without... that the one body you've wrapped your arms around ... the only skin you've ever known... is your own—and that it's dry... and not warm" (p. 169). The only limits which remain intact are those of human mortality, separation, and aloneness. The identification which the audience feels with the characters is not a matter of situation or experience, since those elements are the least realistic elements in the work. Rather, it is an identification based on a mutual feeling of uneasiness and a shared sense of personal vulnerability. Such is the discomfiting message with which the play confronts its audience and critics. A little later, Edna concludes: "finally... there's nothing there... save rust; bones; and the wind" (p. 169).

It is as a protection against this realization that mankind creates his daily patterns, and it is this very realization which demonstrates the brittleness of these fictions. At the end of the play, Agnes says, "They say we sleep to let the demons out—to let the mind go raving mad, our dreams and nightmares all our logic gone awry, the dark side of our reason. And when the daylight comes again... comes order with it" (p. 175). Theatre at its best can accomplish this exorcism by allowing us to participate in "the dark side of our reason" but at a comfortably safe distance. Albee has succeeded in showing us such demons that we may understand better the miracle of *not* becoming a stranger in a world where the foundation of our sense of well-being tends to be sand rather than rock. We can neither rely on the patterns as if they were etched in granite nor can we exist adrift, "strangers in the world, quite uninvolved." Edward Albee has explored this delicate balance in his play and, while disturbing our sense of well-being, has helped us to understand ourselves better.[11]

Notes

[1]Edward Albee, *A Delicate Balance* (New York: Atheneum Pocket Book edition, 1968), p. 65. All subsequent page references appear in the text.

[2] Terence Brown, "Harmonia Discord and Stochastic Process: Edward Albee's *A Delicate Balance*," *re: arts and letters* 3, No. 2 (Spring 1970):54.

[3] John J. von Szeliski, "Albee: A Rare Balance," *Twentieth Century Literature* 16, No. 2 (April 1970):127.

[4] For a survey of reprinted reviews of *A Delicate Balance*, see John Gassner, *Dramatic Soundings: Evaluations Culled from Thirty Years of Dramatic Criticism* (New York: Crown, 1968), pp. 604–7.

[5] Edward Albee, *Tiny Alice* (New York: Atheneum Pocket Book Edition, 1965), p. 60. All subsequent page references appear in the text.

[6] von Szeliski, "Albee," p. 123.

[7] Robert M. Post, "Fear Itself: Edward Albee's *A Delicate Balance*," *C.L.A. Journal* 13, No. 1 (Sept. 1969):167.

[8] C. W. E. Bigsby, *Albee* (Edinburgh: Oliver & Boyd, 1969), p. 98.

[9] von Szeliski, "Albee," p. 130.

[10] Post, "Fear Itself," p. 167.

[11] I would like to thank Professor Sophia Morgan and Mrs. Aladeen Smith for their encouragement and help in the preparation of this essay.

On Death, Dying, and the Manner of Living
Waste as Theme in Edward Albee's
The Lady from Dubuque

E DWARD ALBEE's latest original play, *The Lady from Dubuque*, pro-
voked the sort of critical reaction with which scholars of Albee
theater have become familiar: a great deal of scathing, scornful hostility and somewhat lesser amounts of praise. Even Robert Brustein, who
labeled Albee an "unfortunate man" who has become "the raw flesh of
the American theater," called *The Lady from Dubuque* "an awful piece."[1]
John Simon, self-proclaimed Albeephobe, considerably out-distanced
Brustein by calling the drama "one of the worst plays about anything,
ever."[2] The specific charges against Albee's dramaturgy were familiar
ones: the play lacks unity and coherence; the characters are inhuman,
lacking identity; thematically, the play is an instance of Albee repeating
Albee—badly.[3]

While it is true that *The Lady from Dubuque* focuses on vintage
Albee themes — death, dying, and failed communication among the
living — what makes the play engaging is its focus on how the central
couple, Jo and Sam, ultimately respond to the complex process of living
and dying. Through Sam and the other characters who are brought
into the orbit of Jo's experience of dying, Albee presents a thematic
statement on the manner of living by showing that although Jo's life is
physically about to cease, she radiates more life than do the physically
healthy characters. This is because Jo is not the only character who is
dying. Her companions, long before this play begins, have succumbed
to a debilitating disease which now paralyzes them. Indeed, the

65

spiritual malaise under which they suffer is so complete that *The Lady from Dubuque* is a play whose parts are made coherent by its pervasive dramatization of the theme of waste, for throughout the play one finds an array of wasted relationships, wasted love, and even wasted lives. Albee, himself, has commented on just such waste as an important theme in his works: "I am very concerned with the fact that so many people turn off because it is easier; that they don't stay fully aware during the course of their lives, in all the choices they make: social, economic, political, aesthetic. They turn off because it's easier. But I find that anything less than absolutely full, dangerous participation is an absolute waste of some rather valuable time."[4]

Within *The Lady from Dubuque*, Albee's strategy for the chronicling of such waste is most obviously seen in the two act structure of the play. The first act serves chiefly to introduce and define the principal characters, whose painful vacuity and self-centeredness far. overshadow any claim to individuality which each might make. Because each character becomes merely a hollow variation of a wasted life, the first act also serves to weld these types into a collective, a society of beings brought together through waste and mutual weakness. Yet having firmly established the normative values of this insular gathering, the playwright begins the second act by challenging those values through the introduction of two "alien" characters who are not of the world of the first act. The technique is, of course, an old one for Albee whose introduction of Jerry into Peter's world in *The Zoo Story* and of the Lizard People in *Seascape* achieved much the same effect. Within *The Lady from Dubuque*, these outsiders, by providing Jo with the warmth and compassion that are absent in the first act, present a threat which is ironically more strongly felt than Jo's disease or the sense of mortality which it introduces into the various characters' lives.

Within the play's first act, what becomes most apparent is not only the extreme lack of action but also the lack of interaction as well. Each of the characters speaks for himself but not to the others, so that the game played in the first act appears as a type of play within a play where the players adopt suitably Pirandellian roles of self-conscious characters who explain themselves directly to their supposed audience. Indeed, the characters' preoccupation with defining themselves reflects a major theme of the play since Albee, in a recent interview, indicated that *The Lady from Dubuque* is "all about identity."[5]

The clearest emblem for the type of wasted lives which concern the author is Fred, whose conduct and prejudice reveal his dulled and coarsened sensibility—if, indeed, he can be said to possess sensibilities at all. Foolish enough to be duped by Carol's and Sam's practical joke in which she staves off Sam's feigned entreaties, Fred responds in the only fashion he knows — by physically asserting his presence. When threatened, Fred, according to stage directions, characteristically readies himself "for battle"[6] and resorts to verbal aggression and vulgarity. A few other telling scenes serve to illustrate this point. Near the end of the play, a bound and exasperated Sam screams, prompting Fred to arms so that he punches his friend "hard in the stomach" (p. 146), doubling Sam over in pain. Moments later, Carol decides to have coffee, and Fred, threatened by her show of independence and reluctance to leave with him, "sweeps" the entire coffee service to the floor (p. 147), shattering saucers, cups and any claim to civility which he might have had.

The above examples reveal more than Fred's propensity to assert himself physically. They also suggest that reality is defined for Fred solely in terms of his own self-interest and by his severely limited and bigoted perceptions of the world. He is more pathetic than, say, Eugene O'Neill's Yank, that image of raw, visceral man in *The Hairy Ape*, for the audience could empathize with Yank's noble yet ineffectual struggle to "belong."[7] In contrast, the audience of *The Lady from Dubuque* can only recoil from Fred and his animality. This reaction occurs not because he is—in Jo's words, "just plain dirt common" (p. 23) —but because he treats those around him as objects rather than as human beings. Fred may be perceptive enough to ask, with respect to Sam's and Jo's home, "Where else can you come in this cold world, week after week, as regular as patchwork, and be guaranteed ridicule and contempt?" (p. 30), but he fails to see that *he* is the very one who overflows with these qualities. If his treatment of Carol is any indication, Albee suggests, it is hardly surprising that he has been divorced three times. As Carol testifies, despite whatever sexual fulfillment she finds in Fred, he clearly provides her with little of an emotional or spiritual nature. From the racial slurs with which he accosts Oscar (pp. 106–108) to his physical attack on his host (p. 146), Fred is presented as consistently affirming his self-centeredness. Not once, for instance, does he show compassion for Jo. Rather, he asserts his presence in such an overbearing way that he blinds himself to her plight.

In Albee's presentation, Carol emerges as a practical-minded woman. Carol, described as young and "ripe,"[8] has been involved with Fred and even considers marrying him. She admits her uncertainty about Fred and matrimony; however, she remains confused about the prospect of marriage and thus quells her fear with simplistic reasoning:

"I don't know, I don't know, I don't know! I know it's late and I got the itch [to marry], but beyond that I'm not sure" (p. 38). Lacking in social refinement ["I'm gonna go pee" (p. 28), she publicly announces], Carol seems well-matched with Fred. A woman who dyes her naturally blond hair brunette — "cause I look cheap as a blonde?" (p. 131) — Carol remains a comic figure, breaking certain tense scenes with her matter-of-fact and sometimes humorous lines.

Yet, as a newcomer to the group, Carol enjoys a freedom from the long-established, deadening patterns of the others. Moreover, her role as an "outsider" (p. 124) allows her to comment more honestly about their and her own responses. In certain respects, she is reminiscent of Claire in *A Delicate Balance:* both are outspoken, humorous, and capable of observing the others from a somewhat neutral vantage point —from the "fifty-yard line," as Claire says.[9] Like Claire, however, Carol also succumbs to her own emotional condition and is unable ultimately to better herself.

If Carol is "not your dumb brunette" (p. 131), that is because of her genuine, if limited, ability to be aware of the world around her. Unlike the others, her ego does not prevent her from experiencing the world apart from herself. Her judgment of character is surely flawed, for a relationship with Fred seems earmarked for failure. Still, Carol radiates an openness that distinguishes her from the others and gains for her the audience's sympathy. For example, Carol's only game of the night—her and Sam's practical joke—is truly engaging. It is in marked contrast to the others' identity guessing game of "Twenty Questions" in which Carol chooses not to act out a part. Carol's openness is confirmed in Act Two when she, alone, comes to Sam's defense. While all of the others question Sam's credibility, the newcomer, Carol, counters: "Why doesn't anybody believe *Sam?*" (p. 125); "*Sam* has rights, you know" (p. 134). It is she who finally unties Sam near the close of the play.

For Carol, however, waste looms. This is because her needs are reduced to relatively simple and confining terms. She neither requests nor receives much. If she is open, sharing, and honest, she also fails to improve her predicament, succumbing as she does to Fred's demands. Her obedience to Fred's callous requests—"Fred: Will you get your ass in there [the kitchen]!? Carol: O.K.! O.K.! For Christ's sake!" (p. 125)— foreshadows her final acquiescence to a wasted life, a surrender confirmed when she confides to Elizabeth her reasons for marrying Fred: "He's on his way down hill; he's a barrel of laughs; he's a lush; he's a great fuck; I'm not doing anything else this week; I'm not twenty-two anymore, and I'm scared? Take your choice; they're all true" (p. 151).

For Lucinda and Edgar, the events of the evening represent part of a larger, repetitive routine. As usual, they visit Jo and Sam more out of habit than authentic concern and consequently gain little from the encounter. Albee describes the couple as an "average" pair, and there is little evidence in the action to dispel this description. A former college-mate of Jo, Lucinda has settled into being Edgar's housewife. Polite and quick to observe propriety, she attends to social appearances, interjecting the banal or predictable remark when appropriate. Though Edgar confesses that they have "as much ridicule and contempt as the next house" (p. 31), Lucinda objects—not because they do not battle as George and Martha did in *Who's Afraid of Virginia Woolf?* but simply because they do not communicate "with talk and presence," as the Wife in *All Over* recalls about her early life with her husband.

Lucinda's life, in accordance with her values, has been an untroubled one. Consequently, when Jo berates her, she is hardly equipped to defend her values and convictions. Instead, she yields. For instance, after being ignored and then dismissed as essentially a bore— "Jo: ... You're lucky you've got anybody living in the same *house* with you, much less *talking* to you" (p. 41) — Lucinda loses all emotional control. As Edgar recalls, "Lucinda's down there on the lawn, and she's pulling up tufts of grass and throwing 'em around, and she's got dirt all over her, and I don't think it's any crap" (p. 52). In her opportunity to cut through the cackle and communicate honestly with her dying friend, Lucinda fails, choosing instead to exit and pout. It is her way of asserting that she, not Jo, suffers. And like Fred, she never really attends to Jo. She knows that Jo's derisive behavior stems from a debilitating illness, and yet she bases her forgiveness of Jo, not on genuine care or love, but on a self-centered rationalization: "I'm going to forgive you because I assume that pain is very bad" (p. 42).

Edgar emerges as the most fully sketched of the minor characters. Like Sam, Edgar lives in a comfortable suburb, and, by all indications, he has been an ample provider, a forthright husband. He knows that the others dislike and mock his wife, which finally prompts a defense of his relationship: "I decided a long time ago that the fact that I love Lucinda gives her all the virtue she needs—if there's a lack to begin with" (p. 58). But what distinguishes Edgar is the quality of his awareness regarding Jo's and Sam's predicament, an awareness that goes beyond his acknowledgement that the night "was your nice, average, desperate evening" (p. 43). He emerges as the first character, for instance, who directly confronts Jo about her illness, but he immediately evades further discussion of her condition. He broaches the subject only much later, when, significantly enough, Jo is absent.

Their private dialogue progresses through two distinct stages, the first of which is laced with a series of virulent confrontations. Initially Edgar becomes annoyed, then angry, with Sam's sarcastic, even disrespectful remarks. Pushed to emotional limits, Edgar suddenly explodes: "JESUS CHRIST, WHAT KIND OF HOUSE DO YOU RUN AROUND HERE?" (p. 57). Moments later, he tells his best friend, "You got a whip goes right through cloth, don't you?" (p. 59). Clearly both men are angry, and long suppressed emotions surface. However, their dialogue enters into a second stage, which is characterized by a series of open, honest remarks. Progressing from tension to tonic, in a rare moment of rapport between Edgar and Sam, the two lower their defenses. Edgar offers assistance while Sam declines, reasoning that "nobody can help" (p. 60).

But even here a sense of waste exists, since Edgar, in spite of his levelheadedness and sensitivity, fails to pinpoint the true source of Jo's suffering. For example, rather than talking with Jo about her illness and behavior, Edgar chooses to talk with Sam. Further, his remarks suggest that he is unable or unwilling to understand Jo's actions and the motives which fuel her outbursts. As he abruptly asks Sam: "Can't you control her? Even a little? You let her run wild these days, these nights?" (p. 56). For a well-mannered, rational Edgar, Jo's outbursts are both embarrassing and unacceptable. His concern, it seems, is not so much with Jo as it is with her behavior, with her maintaining a civil, respectable disposition. The sense of waste is correspondingly heightened since the audience comes to expect more from Edgar. The quality of his perceptions, after all, appears sharper, more refined than Fred's, Carol's, and Lucinda's, and therefore the possibility for his fully understanding Jo's plight seems greater. Like the others, however, Edgar is cast as misunderstanding the full nature of Jo's suffering. That he misunderstands only accentuates the wasted potential for authentic communication and love to surface during the evening's encounters.

Both Lucinda and Edgar, accordingly, waste their opportunities to speak honestly with Jo. Like the others, their egotistical and inappropriate responses finally prevent them from sharing warmth and love—the precise form of comforting that Jo craves—or even from distracting Jo from her suffering. Two occurrences confirm this point. The first takes places in Act Two after an offended Edgar recounts how his virtues apparently embarrass Sam. Lucinda responds in a characteristically self-centered reply: "We don't forget, Sam; we may forgive, but we don't forget" (p. 139). Lucinda's statements reveal a selfishness that precludes any genuine understanding of their friends' circumstance. Moreover, their inability to "forget" certain events negates their potential for authentic growth, for it now appears that they will always regard Jo and Sam with rigid, preconceived notions.

The second incident confirming their self-centeredness occurs near the end of the play. In the following passage, Edgar and Lucinda relinquish claims to friendship by abandoning Sam:

Edgar: (*To Sam.*) We came over here to *forgive* you!

Sam: (*Shakes his head; gently.*) It doesn't matter, Edgar.

Edgar: (*Quivering with rage.*) How *dare* you let this happen to you!

Lucinda: (*Realizing it.*) That's right! We came to forgive you!

Sam: (*To stop the exchange.*) It's all right; it doesn't matter.

Edgar: How *dare* you let this happen! I'm not *here* anymore, Sam.

Lucinda: (*Suddenly in tears.*) I never want to come here again! I never want to come to this house again! (*She runs out*).

Edgar: I'm not *here* anymore, Sam.

Sam: (*Pause; accepting.*) O.K., Edgar.

Edgar: (*Sudden contained emotion.*) I'm not here, God damn you! (*Edgar backs into the hall, turns, exits.*) (pp. 150–151).

If Edgar and Lucinda possess any legitimate concern for their friends, they lose it here. Always interpreting experience from *their* own points of view, Edgar and Lucinda are ultimately unable to perceive the needs of their life-long companions. In the hour of Sam's and Jo's collective need, they leave. As the playwright has noted, "Our reality is made up of that which we need at the time we need it, and some people's reality needs can necessarily supersede other people's."[11] Sadly, this, as is all too evident, is the case with Lucinda and Edgar who consistently place a premium on their own needs.

Against this backdrop of the waste and self-centeredness of the supporting cast, Albee presents the barrenness of the lives of the play's central characters. On one level, the evening represents for Jo and Sam merely another social gathering of friends old and new. But on a deeper level, the events of the evening bring out the essence of Jo's and Sam's relationship. Their responses to their guests, to each other, and to themselves, reveal that their lives together have largely been wasted. Jo's imminent death makes such barrenness all the more disheartening. For her, it appears too late to redeem her marriage, in part because her friends and husband offer little support and in part because physical frailty and decay are overtaking her. For Sam, even his wife's dying cannot dislocate his self-serving interests: frailty and decay, on a symbolic level, are overtaking him. By the close of the drama, we learn that their respective "reality needs," as Albee calls them, do at times converge but more often remain at cross-purposes. Through the course of the play, Albee suggests that Jo yearns for love and understanding, desires which Sam apparently cannot fully recognize and fulfill. Waste, then, for this couple, stems not from Jo's physical deterioration and inevitable death, but rather from a crucial breakdown in communication between man and woman, from an inability to salvage qualitatively what scant time remains for Jo.

For Jo, an attractive and perspicacious woman, the gathering of friends for an evening of games and drink is more bothersome than soothing. Moments into the play, she voices her displeasure, expressing both her boredom and disgust with their presence and games: *"(Sarcastically enthusiastic)* 'Yes, and wasn't it boring? Wasn't it all ... empty, ultimately? Didn't we waste our time? *(To the audience; without emotion)* Especially if you're dying, as I am'" (p. 21).

Her friends, respecting though not really understanding her predicament, uphold social appearances and either overlook or endure her remarks. But their well-meaning, if awkward, responses only exacerbate Jo's condition, as is clear when she launches into a litany-like series of coarse rejections: "Fuck New Jersey!" ... "Fuck Jo's mother's sister" ... "Fuck merely trying". ... "Ah, fuck Jo's mother". ... "Fuck furtive blue eyes" (pp. 19–20). Throughout the first act, Albee presents Jo as one who continually vents her frustrations, berating long-time friends one moment and her husband the next. She displays little patience for Fred, whom she calls "a reactionary, Nixon-loving fag baiter" (p. 50), though she accepts Carol: "She's not bad; she's got a good mouth..." (p. 29). The unassertive, complacent Lucinda riles Jo; she tolerates more than enjoys Edgar; and while she loves her husband, ridicule overshadows her care for him. Frustrated by their unwillingness or inability to understand the real source of her suffering, Jo lashes out at everyone, taking comfort in aggressive verbal assaults. Albee portrays her friends, in turn, as failing to comprehend the underlying reasons for her actions, for they think that they must bear with Jo because she is, after all, ill. This is why June Schlueter suggests that in Act One, "We simply accept Jo as a somewhat obnoxious but pitiful woman who, unlike the others, has an excuse for her nastiness."[12]

Sam plays peacemaker in Act One. In trying to placate and make amends for Jo's brusque behavior, he continually explains and clarifies, attempting to smooth over social rough spots. Just as Jo's and Fred's conversation turns into a verbal duel, for instance, Sam intercedes: "Hey come on; I'll think you two like each other" (p. 23). And when Jo again alludes to her dying, Sam pleads: "Come on, Jo. Please?" (p. 21). A handsome forty-year-old, Sam mainly concerns himself with tactfully sustaining social appearances. As Jo sarcastically confides in one of her asides to the audience, "Sam's a great egalitarian; Sam pretends to like everyone equally" (p. 28). In his efforts to please everybody, however, Sam ends up angering his guests and, more importantly, alienating himself from Jo.

Significantly, it is only at the end of Act One that Jo and Sam communicate as if they are truly married. Here husband and wife attend to each other, talking and touching with a sense of commitment behind their deeds. And in their rare moment of rapport, there exists a still rarer expression, in this play, of genuine commitment. The tonal quality of the closing scene of Act One is reminiscent of the rare and loving expressions of care and peace between George and Martha in *Who's Afraid of Virginia Woolf?*. Significantly, during this unique time when Sam displays authentic affection for Jo, she willingly capitulates, relishing the expression of love that has been too long repressed:

Jo: *(Instinctively, they run to each other and embrace.)* Oh, my Sam, my Sam! I'd marry you in a minute!

Sam: *(Picks her up in his arms.)* Shhhh, shhhh, shhhh, shhhh.

Jo: In a minute. *(Cuddle; protected; content.)* Am I heavy? No, of course I'm not heavy. What am I thinking of?

Sam: Shhhh, shhhh, shhhh.

Jo: I think my sleepy pills are working. Shall I go to sleep right here? Can you stand here all night?

Sam: You're not *that* light. I'll take you up. *(He doesn't move, beyond kissing her neck.)* I'll take you to bed (pp. 70–71).

If Sam offers compassionate assistance, then Jo gladly receives it. Moreover, at this juncture, Sam is presented as one still in control; it is still his house and Jo remains within his influence.

And yet the closing moments of Act One also anticipate Sam's ultimately wasteful stance towards living. For example, he reasons that, as Jo dies, he must respond to the loss by holding "on to the object we're losing" (p. 61). Reflecting on the meaning of her death, Sam seems unable to accept the reality of non-being. He clings selfishly to Jo "the object" to the extent that she becomes spiritually manacled by her husband. Importantly enough, the period in which Jo is most free in the play occurs when Sam is physically bound with a rope. The sense of waste becomes accentuated by his inability to distinguish between differing forms of bondage —the kind Jo experiences *versus* the kind he endures. And the psychological damage caused by Sam's refusal to allow Jo or himself, in Albee's words, to "exhibit too much 'relatable' pain — psychologically"[13] fosters a profound sense of estrangement. In this light, Sam does as much damage to the relationship as does Jo's physical disease. He reacts with hostility when shackled, just as Jo, in Act One, reacts with hostility when symbolically shackled. Sam, like his friends, clings to "the object" he is losing because he can neither face up to nor comprehend death. Sam even appears emotionally paralyzed at times: Jo howls in agony while Sam stands and "watches," unable to react on any level (p. 51). Soon after, she talks about the illness, only to meet with Sam's evasions: "We can't just talk about it [her illness], it's that simple.... No. No. I don't want to hear them [Jo's report on two medical theories, one of which seems to be that of Kübler-Ross]" (p. 68). Like so many Albee characters, Sam avoids confronting painful truths.

In the end, Albee seems to suggest that the evening of drinks and games occurs more to satisfy Sam's desires than to sooth Jo's pains. At best, the evening simply represents a distraction from Jo's suffering as well as from his own inability to confront directly the reality of her dying. Like Praskovya in Leo Tolstoy's "The Death of Ivan Ilych," Sam translates Jo's misery into how *he* must endure such pain. Oscar illuminates this point when he rightly inquires: "What does Sam know? Sam only knows what *Sam* needs.... And what about what Jo needs? What does what Sam needs have to do with that?" (p. 134). The point is, of course, that what Sam needs has little bearing on what Jo requires. Jo is certainly aware of the considerable distance between their "reality needs," as seen when she wryly asks Sam: "Your pain's as bad as mine, eh?" (p. 62). Despite Sam's attempt to avoid the question, the audience realizes the accuracy of Jo's inquiry. For Jo, on the other hand, the events of the evening represent yet another wasted opportunity for her companions to discern her needs accurately. Thus, on this night she can only vent her anger and disappointment. Since Sam cannot or will not provide succor and since her mother has yet to help, she takes comfort in her aggressive verbal assaults.[14]

Jo and especially Sam are, then, in many ways a suitable nucleus for the society which has gathered around them, reflecting as they do so many of its values and wasteful tendencies. However, as has already been noted, Act Two disrupts the social order which is so carefully established in the first part of the play. In what might loosely be called a borrowing of the Romance device of the outsider whose entrance serves as a simultaneous threat to order and a call to adventure, Albee shatters the self-congratulation and complacency of the first act through the introduction of the outsiders, Elizabeth and Oscar. Functioning much like the White Rabbit who disrupts the well established order of Alice's Victorian environs, the two strangers in *The Lady from Dubuque* lead a disbelieving Sam into a wonderland where the laws of time and space and logic established in the first part of the play are no longer in force, a world in which Elizabeth from New Jersey can be Jo's mother from Dubuque.

As denizens of the world beyond the tightly circumscribed realm of Sam's and Jo's living room, Elizabeth and Oscar are markedly different from the regular habitues of the house. Elizabeth is a "stylish, elegant, handsome woman" and much of her stunning presence emerges from two contrasts. First, she is markedly different from the other characters, radiating a mysterious as well as sophisticated air. Patrician, eloquent, and a world traveller, her deportment acts as a counterpoint to the more common and, at times, raucous behavior of the other characters. Secondly, Elizabeth subverts the audience's as well as the other characters' expectations regarding her actual identity. That is, throughout the first act Jo's mother is described as a small, thin woman with "furtive blue eyes" and "pale hair, tainted pink, balding a little" (p. 20). With stylish hat and fur cloak, Elizabeth hardly resembles Sam's description of his mother-in-law and emerges as anything but the less cultured woman that her hometown title/name is, according to some critics, meant to suggest. [15] Coupled with Oscar, her black confidant who is as debonair and composed as she is urbane and commanding, Elizabeth is set to usurp Sam's authority.

That usurpation is achieved by the making over of Sam's world into an abstract looking glass world where everything is parodically made over or reversed with the result that there is a dynamic tension created by the simultaneous similarity and difference between the second act and what has come before. Thus Act One opens with a series of questions, and Albee again uses this technique although with changes at the outset of the second act. Sam is quite serious in his exchange with the intruders, and this question-and-answer scene clearly mirrors the game of Twenty Questions which Sam delighted in playing the night before — much to his discomfort now. Fixed on Elizabeth and Oscar, Sam relentlessly probes, as his friends had done regarding his identity in the game of Twenty Questions, "Who AAAR-RRRE you!?" (p. 76).

When Jo correctly guesses his identity in Twenty Questions in Act One, Sam sulks, rationalizing that she did not play *his* game fairly. These early moments are important in two respects. First, as the guessing game in Act One was not, according to Sam, fairly played, just as the real-life game in Act Two, from Sam's point of view, will not be fairly played. Secondly, as Sam fails to handle defeat maturely in a simple guessing game, so he will fail later to handle defeat maturely in the most serious game of his life when Jo necessarily separates from his world. This foreshadowing of Sam's weakness of character and ultimate loss of control is also evident in his offhand confession that he dislikes Jo's mother (p. 20). Sam, outwardly the one who enjoys everybody's company, emerges as the one who inwardly closes down to those who do not fit with the scheme of his desires and needs. Finally, even the true identity of Elizabeth matters little to Sam because Albee presents him as rejecting anyone who unfavorably encroaches on his world.

In Albee's presentation of Sam's world, there is no real sharing of the self with the other. Consistently in Act Two, his immediate and steadfast concern is not with aiding but with prompting her to deny the identity of the nemesis who threatens his sense of propriety and order: "This woman claims to be your mother. Tell her, Jo; tell her you don't know her. ... Tell her she has no right to come into our home and pretend to be what she is not" (p. 116). By insistently pursuing his own rights, Sam spoils their last hours together.

Jo instinctively knows this. The intensity of her sarcasm in Act One is a measure of her loss. Her responses stem not only from an awareness of the impending loss of her own life, but also from the realization that her relationship with Sam has deteriorated into a non-marriage. With the support of Elizabeth the outsider, Jo is able to confirm and accept her husband's beliefs, beliefs which are emotionally understandable in context but which also preserve their non-marriage. Thus, Elizabeth and Oscar allow Jo and force Sam to re-define their reality. And to re-define their relationship in authentic terms is to unmask the lack of love between them. As Elizabeth confides to Jo: "He wasn't happy with the way things are. He wanted everything back the way it never was" (p. 133). Though nearly comatose in the above exchange, Jo nevertheless recognizes the truth of Elizabeth's statements.

Jo detects and is attracted to the truth and comfort afforded by Elizabeth and Oscar. From the outset, Albee indicates that Jo is not satisfied, and one can locate the source of much of her dissatisfaction in her confession that her mother never helped during the illness:

"Where is she? Where the hell is she? ... YEAH! IN THE HOUR OF MY GODDAMN NEED!!" (p. 18). Elizabeth's announcement that she is Jo's mother thus establishes her as a crucial figure in Jo's world. But her true identity is irrelevant. The others are confused by this; Sam refuses to accept it; but whether or not Elizabeth actually is Jo's mother is subordinate to the *role* she plays, to the comfort she provides, and to the love she shares. The audience knows that Elizabeth is not Jo's mother, and a clearheaded Jo would surely know it too.

But Jo is dying. Her rational faculties, clouded by pain-dampening drugs and her body's decay, give way to emotional needs, needs that Elizabeth and Oscar satisfy. Albee's imagery gives shape to Jo's present state of being. For example, in contrast to Act One, her responses in Act Two are described as being "Timid" (p. 117), "Dreamy" (p. 127), "Vague" (p. 142), and "Faint" (p. 147)—words which, in context, evoke death-like images. Nearing death, Jo's movements become hesitant, her utterances feeble. Like Sam, she is clothed in a sleeping gown as she begins her "descent" (p. 116) towards the living room and towards her dying-room.

Dr. Elisabeth Kübler-Ross, in her *On Death and Dying*, suggests that as one approaches death, one experiences an increasing need for sleep "very similar to that of the newborn child."[16] Jo not only lapses into longer periods of sleep, but the quality of her voice actually shifts into a childlike tone when Elizabeth cuddles her. Lured by the protection offered by the lady from Dubuque, Jo converses as "A little girl" (p. 118), giving herself over as a child to a mother. Albee's stage direction is emphatic: "Finally, with tears and a great helpless smile, Jo rushes into Elizabeth's arms; their embrace is almost a tableau, so involved is it with pressing together" (p. 118).

If Elizabeth functions as a loving mother-figure to Jo, she also represents, paradoxically, a less-meaningful relationship, since Albee traces the psychological reactions that a dying person experiences, and Jo necessarily prepares for death by gradually detaching herself from loved ones. Kübler-Ross suggests that it is a complex process, one usually met with misunderstanding. As Kübler-Ross observes with respect to a family's reactions to one who, like Jo, is on the brink of death, "They [the family members] do not understand that a dying man who has found peace and acceptance in his death will have to separate himself, step by step, from his environment, including his most loved ones."[17] Jo finds herself in the midst of the final stages leading to her death, when near the end of the play, she is separating herself from Sam and her familiar surroundings.[18] Elizabeth and Oscar provide a necessary compromise between the total involvement with living and the total cessation of existence. Like all such other-worldly romance guides, they provide a pathway to a displaced world beyond or, at the least, a different state of being. Albee presents the process of Jo's transition in its full complexity: "Jo *(Detached):* Well, I dare say the day will come I'll need you all. Then, of course, the day will come I won't need a soul. And then, of course, the day won't come.... That's what they tell us, isn't it—that growing pile of books on how to die? That somewhere along the line you stop needing those you...need the most? You loose your ties? God, what do you need then?" (p. 47). Thus, in making the transition to the other world of Elizabeth and Oscar, what is left behind are the many "needs" which so dominate the first act of the play.

In direct contrast to Jo's letting go and abandoning of the world which she has known, Sam tries to maintain the *status quo* by tenaciously claiming "rights" to his dearest possessions: Jo and home. In the hour of Jo's need, Sam appears unable to help precisely because of his stubborn belief in "rights." Sam mistakenly thinks that he can lay claim to, and have control over, Jo's emotions. Like Peter's claim to the park bench in *The Zoo Story,* Sam's claim to his possessions reduces him to a pathetic figure, one who perceives Jo and home as bits of "property" (p. 145). And as Peter's claim leads to his demise, so Sam's contributes to his fall, for Albee has Sam experience the world around him solely from his own point of view. His rights, Elizabeth points out, remain his and have nothing to do with Jo's (p. 144).

Characteristically, Jo's acceptance of Elizabeth and Oscar is interpreted by Sam as a mark of rejection, resulting in his loss of control. For now, he must abdicate his power, his possessions, his "rights." Oscar now dresses like Sam, utters some of Sam's previous lines and, indeed, assumes Sam's former role as both protector and comforter. Elizabeth and Oscar create an illusion that assuages Jo's pain, which Sam finally comes to realize: *"(Chilling knowledge):* 'Is that [i.e., Jo's needs] what matters'?" (p. 154). In a final, desperate effort to communicate with his wife, Sam still does not fully comfort her. Despite Jo's pleas for compassion and understanding, Sam reverts again to defining reality from his own reference point. Declaring that he is "not any part of" Jo's world anymore (p. 156) and asserting that it is he who is "dying" (p. 155), Sam assures both Jo and himself of a wasted life together.

In several of Albee's plays, the characters come to realize the possibility for spiritual regeneration. This motif appears, for instance, in such works as *Who's Afraid of Virginia Woolf?*, *A Delicate Balance*, and *Seascape*. However, such is not the case in *The Lady from Dubuque* because the characters remain incapable of seeking out a limited but palpable hope for a new understanding, a new perception of reality. Fred and Carol, with Edgar and Lucinda, retreat into their familiar habits, unchanged—or only embittered—by their recent experience. Elizabeth and Oscar, probably messengers of death, perform their duty and, with Jo's death, will simply take leave. Sam—unlike Peter in *The Zoo Story*, George and Martha in *Who's Afraid of Virginia Woolf?*, or even Charlie in *Seascape*—learns little about love and the self from his encounters. He sees the help Elizabeth and Oscar give Jo but quickly loses sight of that comfort and returns to his self-centeredness. With his guests, he remains as dead as the Romulus and Remus figures in the game of Twenty Questions. They have long conducted themselves as if they were "The very dead; who hear nothing; who remember nothing; who are nothing" (p. 138).

Here, then, lies the irony of the drama. Death is a ubiquitous force, encompassing not only Jo's literal death but also including figuratively the death of her friends and husband. All the physically healthy characters, with the exceptions of Elizabeth and Oscar, conduct themselves as if they were anesthetized to both their inner and outer worlds. They have fallen to the "sin" to which the Girl in Albee's *Listening* refers: "We do not have to live unless we wish to; the greatest sin in living is doing it badly...stupidly, as if you were not alive."[19] For various reasons and to various degrees, the characters in *The Lady from Dubuque* have existed "as if [they] were not alive." The central theme of waste emerges because the characters have responded mostly to their own suffering and concerns and to their own fractured relationships. Except for Elizabeth and Oscar, and perhaps Carol, all seem to have difficulties attending to the world outside themselves. Even the grey-colored interior of the setting appropriately captures the bleakness of the characters' inner existences.

Finally, the presence of death allows Sam to confront his real self and allows him the opportunity to participate in life honestly and compassionately—what Albee called a "full, dangerous participation" in experience—which is essential if the spirit is to re-awaken. As Albee has observed: "I am concerned with being as self-aware as we possibly can be and staying as alert and involved as we possibly can. Being awake, self-aware, and open to all kinds of experience on its own terms —I think those conditions, given half a chance, will produce better self-government, a better society, a better everything else."[20]

That Sam and the others apparently do not accept this kind of immersion into daily encounters — "staying as alert and involved as [they] possibly can"—confirms the wastefulness of their lives. If there is hope for a redemptive force, perhaps it lies with the audience whose perceptions about the manner of living may be altered by the spectacle.[21] That it is too late for Sam and company to change does not lessen the importance, Albee suggests, of such self-awareness.

Notes

[1]Robert Brustein, "Self-Parody and Self-Murder," *The New Republic*, 8 March 1980, p. 26.

[2]John Simon, "From Hunger, Not Dubuque," *New York*, 11 February 1980, p. 74.

[3]Walter Kerr, "Stage: Edward Albee's 'Lady from Dubuque,'" *The New York Times*, 1 February 1980, C-5, contended that Albee "failed to give his on-stage mannequins any actual identities to uncover. We're shooting at zeroes," while Howard Kissel declared that "you never sense human beings beneath them [the words of the dialogue]," in *"The Lady from Dubuque," Women's Wear Daily*, 1 February 1980; rpt. *New York Theatre Critic's Reviews*, ed. Joan Marlowe and Betty Blake, 41(1980). p. 384. According to Edwin Wilson, Albee's action is disunified because "he has let too many extraneous elements get in his way" ("Theater: Edward Albee's 'The Lady from Dubuque,'" *The Wall Street Journal*, 8 February 1980; rpt. *New York Theatre Critic's Reviews*, p. 388). June Schlueter argued that "the problem with *The Lady from Dubuque* is not that Albee has said what has already been said—Beckett, after all, keeps repeating himself—but simply that, in dramatic terms, he has not said it effectively" ("Is It 'All Over' for Edward Albee? *The Lady from Dubuque*," in *Edward Albee: Planned Wilderness*, ed. Patricia De La Fuente [Edinburgh, Texas: Pan American University Press, Living Author Series No. 3, 1980], p. 115). Jack Kroll, who believed that it was "all over," wrote that "the air of the theatre seemed scorched by a negative charge, the electrocution of creative force" ("Going to Hell with Edward Albee," *Newsweek*, 11 February 1980, p. 102). Favorable assessments included Douglas Watt's judgment that the play was, ultimately "compelling" ("Albee on the Chill of Death and Loss," *New York Daily News*, 1 February 1980; rpt. *New York Theatre Critic's Reviews*, p. 385). Clive Barnes observed that "the strength of the play is to be found in the irony and coarseness of the writing, the verbal clarity, the ivory turn of phrase, and, most important of all, in Albee's bone-dry, distilled-ice-cold compassion for human frailty" ("Albee's 'Lady' is Something to Talk About," *The New York Post* 1 February 1980, p. 33). Gerald Clark even claimed that the play represented Albee's "best since *Who's Afraid of Virginia Woolf?* nearly eighteen long years ago" ("Theater-Night Games: *The Lady from Dubuque*," *Time*, 11 February 1980, p. 69).

[4]Matthew C. Roudané, "An Interview with Edward Albee," *Southern Humanities Review* 16 (1982):41.

[5]Roudané, pp. 39–40.

[6]Edward Albee, *The Lady from Dubuque* (New York: Atheneum, 1980), p. 33. All subsequent page references appear in the text.

[7]Eugene O'Neill, *Anna Christie, The Emperor Jones, The Hairy Ape* (New York: Vintage Books, 1972), pp. 172, 230–232.

[8]This description of Carol, along with those of Sam and Jo as well as Elizabeth, is taken from the author's unpaginated descriptions of the characters given at the beginning of the play.

[9]Edward Albee, *A Delicate Balance* (New York: Atheneum, 1966), p. 72.

[10]Edward Albee, *All Over* (New York: Atheneum, 1971), p. 19.

[11]Roudané, p. 41.

[12]Schlueter, p. 116.

[13]Roudané, p. 40.

[14]See Elisabeth Kübler-Ross, M.D., *On Death and Dying* (New York: Macmillan, 1969; rpt. in paperback ed., 1970), pp. 50–57. According to Kübler-Ross, who Albee says influenced the composition of *The Lady from Dubuque*, the dying person progresses through various stages as he or she approaches death. The second stage appears when the patient is filled with "anger, rage, and resentment." This seems to account for Jo's capriciousness in Act One, for, as Sam and company discover, her "anger is displaced in all directions and projected onto the environment at times almost at random."

[15]Kroll states that "'The Lady from Dubuque' is the famous phrase of Harold Ross of *The New Yorker,* who defined his sophisticated magazine by saying that it wasn't for her," p. 103; Clarke concurs: "Her title is derived from Harold Ross's famous statement that he was not editing *The New Yorker* for 'the little old lady in Dubuque,'" p. 388.

[16]Kübler-Ross, p. 112.

[17]Kübler-Ross, p. 170.

[18]For Jo, the anger of Act One yields to the resignation of Act Two. She instinctively realizes that she must lose friends, home, husband, and, finally, the self. Because of her awareness of the impending loss, Sam and friends become less important in her life. They, it seems, interpret this as a mark of disrespect or non-love when it is, according to Kübler-Ross, the mark of a psychological process—that of *decathexis,* or separation, which Jo necessarily experiences. See Kübler-Ross, pp. 119, 170, 176.

[19]Edward Albee, *Counting the Ways and Listening* (New York: Atheneum, 1977), p. 110.

[20]Roudané, p. 43.

[21]When questioned about the relationship between dramatic form and the play's effect on the audience, Albee said,

> When I'm writing a play, I am so involved with the absolute, three-dimensional, literal reality of what I'm doing that I don't concern myself with the metaphor, with the resonance, the symbolism of the play. I am concerned with creating the people and their environment. When I am done with the piece, I'm aware of how it relates to certain things that I feel deeply about—the dishonesty with which people live their lives, perhaps—but not while I'm doing it.
>   I do expect the dramatic experience to have an effect on people. The very best dramatic experiences would change people's perceptions both about themselves and the art form. You expect that to happen, and you hope that that's going to happen when you do something. But while you're doing it, you've *got* to be involved in the reality of it (Roudané, pp. 29–30).

Tiny Alice
The Expense of Joy
in the Persistence of Mystery

LEONARD CASPER

W HEN EDWARD ALBEE was asked by his publisher to provide a
preface for *Tiny Alice* which would explain its peculiarities, he at
first consented; then recanted, having decided that "the play is quite
clear."[1] Further, he declared that even more people shared his view
than found his work obscure. Among the latter, however, were those
daily reviewers who had the most immediate access to the Geilgud-Worth
production in the Billy Rose Theater: Taubman of the *Times,* Kerr of
the *Herald-Tribune,* Watts of the *Daily Post,* and Chapman of the *Daily
News.*[2] The bafflement of such otherwise friendly critics perhaps was
epitomized best by contradictory reviews which appeared in *Time* early
in 1965. The first, on January 8, referred to the play as a "tinny
allegory," dependent more on mystification than mystery; more on
echolalia than on eloquence; more on pretentious reprise of Nietz-
schean nihilism than on profound, fresh inquiry. Only one week later,
the same source was at least willing, half-facetiously, to take part in the
controversial deciphering of *Tiny Alice* by suggesting that meaning
might lie dormant in such apparent clues as references to a "homosex-
ual nightmare," Julian the Apostate, and cunning old Fury's decision in
Alice's Adventures in Wonderland to try poor Mouse with intent to con-
demn him to death for lack of anything better to do that day.

Aside from agit-prop plays, whose ideological direction is
extensively detailed, most plays submit to risks of misunderstanding
involved in the indirection of their argument. But *Tiny Alice* has con-

83

tinued to be considered exceptionally difficult. Even critics who have
tried to admire it have shown signs of testiness, undergoing trials
originating at times in their own ingenuity. Harold Clurman, one of the
earliest, was willing to say that he saw an allegory in which "the pure
person in our world is betrayed by all parties," themselves corrupt.
"Isolated and bereft of every hope, he must die—murdered." But the
result, somehow, reminded him of a Faustian drama written by "a
highly endowed college student."[3] Later and more elaborately, Anne
Paolucci described *Tiny Alice* as "the most impressive of Albee's
paradoxical affirmations of negation."[4] To be consistent with this conclusion, she was compelled to treat the play as an intricate allegory: the
three agents of Alice, for example, compose a sinister "unholy trinity"
concelebrating a parodic ritual of faith; the play is an extended enactment of the smaller scale sexual-spiritual abandon/abandonment experienced by Julian in the asylum. It is a confession of despair: the
Invisible Presence is, in fact, an Immense Absence. Ruby Cohn's version of the play was similarly bleak, finding its central struggle in the
wilful resistance of Julian's imagination to his pronounced desire for
the real. A ceremony is contrived, to wed him to reality: "and even then
he tries to rearrange it into familiar appearance." In the moment of
death, Julian experiences "the prototypical existential confrontation"[5]
—complete isolation; but unable to bear it, invokes Christian allusions/
illusions. Presumably, according to Cohn's version, reality = death =
abstraction = Tiny Alice = self-negation. In her judgment, a man of
true integrity should face this Absurdity with courage, not cower as
Julian does, regressing to childhood. Michael Rutenberg's decoding of
Albee's allegory perceived a diabolic force bartering a billion ordinary
souls for one especially sensitive and worth corrupting, even as the
visible conspirators form a chorus half-sympathetic with the victim.[6]
Although Rutenberg had to admit the ambiguity of the ending, however interpreted, Julian is lost—to Nothingness; or to an Evil Deity; or
to a benevolent but all-devouring God. Positive projections of the
ending have been rarer, perhaps because they have been considered
too naive by the critical mind. And all have ignored the possibility that
any definitive reading is too narrow for Albee.

But suppose *Tiny Alice* resists being treated as allegory because
its meaning lies in the persistence, rather than the resolution, of mystery. Suppose risk, natural to reconnoitering the previously undiscov-
ered or unexplored, is being offered as itself the supreme reality.
Suppose *Tiny Alice* is a tribute to finite man's terrifying instinct for

infinity. The play has at least two structural elements which provide a degree of stability to dimensions otherwise often in flux: the central presence of Julian and the strategic placement of visions at the climax of each of the three acts. As visions deriving from the virginal Julian, they are, of course, suspect. Two of them are even placed offstage and can therefore readily be dismissed as hallucinations in a disturbed mind. Albee offers no clear persuasion of his own but only suggests how best to submit to the play's passions and impressions: "Brother Julian is in the same position as the audience. He's the innocent. If you see things through his eyes, you won't have any trouble at all."[17] Or, perhaps, just the trouble appropriate to flawed and still falling man — trouble not wholly distinguishable from the gift of choice to the half-informed.

When towards the end of Act I Julian reveals to Miss Alice his principal memory of all the six hermitic years spent sealed in an asylum, he cannot declare that it was not something wholly imagined. He had withdrawn so far from external realities that what he relates could have been pure fantasy rather than fabulous consummation. *Was* there an introverted woman who claimed to be the Virgin Mary? *Did* he ejaculate in ecstatic union with her? *Did* she become pregnant with the Son of God as a result? Julian's doctor advises him that some hallucinations are healthy and desirable: clearly *he* knows the difference between mystic insight and self-delusion. He informs Julian flatly that the woman died later of cancer of the womb. Julian, however, remains stricken with wonder.

The strangeness of this tale uncorroborated by onstage enactment, in addition to Julian's own indecisiveness about its nature, authorizes the greatest possible skepticism towards the play's final moments as a prelude to any Ultimate Vision. Are faith and sanity really one, as Julian declares? Or is his final submission, his passionate utterances of faith, a sign of a man now totally mad? Earlier, in Act III, Lawyer has been completely cynical about the consolations of self-delusion: Any man will "take what he gets for...what he wishes it to be. AH, it is what I have always wanted, he'll say, looking terror and betrayal right in the eye. Why not face the inevitable and call it what you have always wanted? How to come out on top, going under" (p. 148). According to the testimony of his own recollections, Julian has always associated sexual desire, death and union with God, in incongruous sublimation. Is that not how he sees the culmination of his life, with self-induced grace that eases the agony of the human condition? Is his vision not voided; any thought of his sanctification not sacrilegious? Are such inversions not to be expected in Alice's Wonderland; such nihilism not inevitable in an Absurdist play?

But the sweet simplicity of that conclusion fails to account for the other vision at the end of Act II, which is unquestionably of the flesh, as naked to the eye as any revelation can be and, therefore, far from hallucinatory. It is precisely the very real presence of Miss Alice which makes possible serious consideration of *Tiny Alice* as an argument that things visible *may* be evidence of things invisible. The tableau in which Miss Alice offers herself as a transparency through which Alice can be seen might easily serve as illustration for Platonic Ideals or Christian Incarnation.

That so traditional a notion could be entertained by Albee should not be disquieting.[8] From the beginning, his plays have complained about the decline of such "ancient verities" (to use Faulkner's words) as family cohesiveness, community life, and continuity in the history of evolving civilization.[9] The Grandmother figure in the early one-act plays represents all of these ideals—as does George, on a more intellectual plane, in *Who's Afraid of Virginia Woolf?*. *Tiny Alice* provides dimensions that infinitely expand the dream/hope that there is more to life than our day-to-day living may signify. One begins to feel less ill at ease with *Tiny Alice* the moment one releases Albee from the box of Absurdism/defeatism where his techniques—the linkage of humor and horror, the seeming cross purposes and discontinuities—invited earlier critics to imprison him. For Albee such mannerisms are, simultaneously, metaphors for the dissipation of faith in meaningfulness and untraditional measures for reinvoking, resurrecting, reconstructing traditions at their best.

Albee does distinguish—again, like Faulkner—between dead convention and living tradition, between inflexible institutions and an order of growth congenial with diversity of direction and possibility. Daddy, in *The Sandbox* and *The American Dream,* is a figure of impotence, his human tracts having been replaced by tubes. Nick, in *Who's Afraid of Virginia Woolf?*, seems to epitomize health and youthful promise, but his proposed eugenics, a form of self-propagation, is indistinguishable from Daddy's living death. In *Tiny Alice,* the Church, represented by the most venal, most self-inflating aspect of the Cardinal, becomes one more Establishment mechanism for deadening human sensibilities.

Beyond its attempt to revitalize traditions of activated faith, *Tiny Alice* more subtly recognizes that the God-ache suffered by man is

foremost an outcry to be born free but not abandoned. The play
provides a continuous experience, rather than a philosophical discussion, of two profoundly permanent problems: how can man imagine
the incommensurate (but we think we do), and how can man separate
service from servitude (but we think we must)? Is there a discernible
point beyond which the search for self in the other annihilates either
that other or one's self? Can self-centeredness be transcended, yet
selfhood be fulfilled? If we attempt to think of an unknowable unknown — such as God — do we delude ourselves more by conjuring
anthropomorphic images or by approximating an abstraction of perfection? Do we earn an afterlife only by refusing to want one? Such are
the dilemmas torturing the mind that aspires to be, become, belong
and, especially, to define beyond desire.

    Tiny Alice is replete with talk of serving. The Cardinal and
Lawyer are, to a large extent, self-serving; so is Miss Alice, inasmuch as
she finds a joy beyond pleasure in Julian's company; and even Butler
often delights in comforting this unfortunate novice beyond the call of
duty. Something of self is retained by all these four agents of causes/
missions larger than themselves. Is this their flaw, or even in the worst
of them is this some sign of grace, of a superior love that allows them a
measure of freedom from complete depersonalization? Does omnipo-
tence require impotence? In the last scenes, do not all these agents act
out that love — though with varying degrees of reluctance — in their
compassion for Julian? Or does their similarity lie in their failing to rise
above self-pity mirrored in another's pain?

    The question deepens when applied to Brother Julian himself.
Early in the play he tells Butler that he committed himself to an asylum
for six years because he was paralyzed by his inability to reconcile his
own view of God, as creator and mover, with the popular view of God as
a kind of miracle-worker on call. With Miss Alice he manages to be
more open and confesses to having been impatient with God and
excessively proud of his humility, as a lay brother in the pretended
service of the Lord. Even now he wishes not to be forgotten for
whatever services he renders; not to be unborn, in death. Miss Alice
accuses him of still more ambition — negotiating martyrdom — and he
admits that his unrelenting dream has been "To go bloodstained and
worthy ... upward" (p. 124). Immediately afterwards, she leads him
from the ecstasy of that memory, to the sacrifice of himself, and to Alice
through her own body.

    Is this climatic moment of Act II the seduction of his soul or an
advanced stage in its salvation? Julian wants his marriage to end in Miss

88 CASPER

Alice. It is required of him, however, that he not confuse symbol with substance, as the Cardinal regularly does. When Julian persists, despite Miss Alice's assurance that "I am the...illusion" (p. 167), he is executed by Lawyer. Julian feels forsaken by God as well as by those departing the scene. Finally, accepting his destiny, provided it is not eternal death, he prays in desperation: "Then Come and Show Thyself! Bride? God?" (p. 189). Lights move through the model/replica of the mansion; sounds approach, in rhythm with his heartbeat. Total darkness descends.

Has this entire drama been a hallucination in the mind of a recluse become catatonic? Has Julian finally married him*self*? Or has his role merely served as insane filter, discoloring the reality of the others? Has this, after all, been a downfall into the void? Can one reconcile Albee's candid admission that "There are some things in the play that are not clear to me"[10] with his assertion that if one positions himself in Julian's place, the play is as clear as need be/can be?

To argue that the direct vision of Miss Alice at the end of Act II may validate the reported visions that, respectively, climax the other acts still acknowledges ambiguities enough to satisfy many an alternate version of *Tiny Alice*'s meaning(s). Remembering Albee's bitter resentment of his abandonment two weeks after birth by his natural parents and his often unhappy childhood with his adoptive parents, one might be inclined to see as pure autobiographical projection this play about a She-God who gives life, only to demand its sacrificial return.[11] Beyond the possibility that all this is personal complaint, problems that are more universal remain. Lawyer remarks in II,2 that God is an abstraction which therefore can neither be understood nor worshipped; whereas Alice, "the mouse in the model" (p. 107), *can* be understood and worshipped, although it does not exist. What does existence mean, here? Does Alice have no permanent reality, no true substance, being only an exotic mask of God? Or is Alice a manifestation, a function of the Godhead, a further stage in man's adventuring towards divinity? Or is Lawyer, in his bitterness/limited knowledge, just distorting the truth? Are Lawyer, Butler and Miss Alice agents of a malignant surrogate God, and are all of them hyenas, scavengers of the dead vitals of men? Are they impure agents in prolonged process of purgation (Butler too still prefers Miss Alice to Alice) of a merciful and loving God or merely "angels of death," imperfect companions to those chosen for possible perfection? Is Alice, like the son in *Who's Afraid of Virginia Woolf?*, invented out of desperate human need to be part of, instead of apart from, some lasting meaning? Is Julian, secretly dedicated to his own destruction by denying that God may be gentle, courting death disguised as a demanding deity? Is his attraction to Miss Alice only a brief interlude in his inevitable marriage to darkness?

Or is this a parable of grace, one more fortunate fall? Does Brother Julian lose his celibacy but gain proper priesthood? The name "Alice" derives from the Greek word for truth. Suppose Butler (the working class) once thought he possessed her; so, more recently, did Lawyer (law makers and stewards of justice). But what single system can speak for the whole Truth? The Church (Miss Alice as "missal"?) and, certainly, individual churchmen have their own insufficiencies; there are cobwebs in the chapel. Julian himself is no chaste Adam, as his childhood fantasies prove, and he falls again—not into the flesh, which has been sanctified by the Incarnation, but into a denial that flesh is symbol rather than substance. He becomes a proper man of God, not in retreat (the asylum) but in the world, in communion. Julian has equated faith and sanity, but at last he accepts the mystery, terror and all beyond reason and historic revelation and rituals that become routine. His uncertainty becomes his cause; he makes the desperate but not despairing mystic leap. Is it implied that we are all called to be Marys whose wombs bring God into his world and the delirious world to its destinate groom? All called but few chosen? And of those chosen, even fewer who reach supreme parturition? Or is such speculation itself not pretending to provide the sort of single-system answer which the general explication set out to refute?

If one could appeal to the rest of Albee's work in this dilemma, the probability is that he would align himself with those who see *Tiny Alice* as a determined quest for spiritual coordinates, for opportunities to convert chance into choice and so to collaborate with life against one's own loneliness and that of others. In his first four one-act plays, Albee implied that we try to compensate for our incompleteness by neglecting the needs of others, although, ironically, the only human strength lies in mutual aid among the weak. Albee at first wrote angrily because he resisted adding to the alienation and displacement and deprivation which some of his predecessors and peers considered *the* human condition. Those plays, like the violent act of Jerry in *The Zoo Story*, were cruel blows intended kindly. The same indignation and hope for reform, though presented with less grotesque humor, persist in *All Over*, one of whose attendants at a wake finally recognizes how they have wasted their lives, how corpselike *they* are: "All we've done is think about ourselves." In *The Lady from Dubuque,* when the dying woman receives little solace from her husband who is overconcerned with himself, she has to turn to the kindness of strangers.[12]

The surface of such plays to the contrary, Albee has been less death- than dream-haunted: by the dream of a bond beyond bondage, a love that allows privacy but not loneliness. In *A Delicate Balance* a plague drives one family into the house of a friend, who then must decide if they have as much right to remain as his own daughter, who wants them out. Tobias the husband delays, reminded of his own terrors by those of his friends, and when they finally leave, he knows that an opportunity to live generously and even expansively has been lost. The bonding of characters in *Who's Afraid of Virginia Woolf?* is more successful because not only is their reliance on one another renewed, but, in Nick and Honey's willingness to bear children, their passion for (re)generation is satisfied vicariously. The same sense of compatibility and continuity, the same ready submission to growth, flourishes in *Seascape* between different species in the same global enterprise.

Early and late, Albee's plays have sprung from a faith remote from both nihilism at one extreme and romanticism at the other. Like Eugene O'Neill before him, he knows the variety of dimensions in dreaming: they can be destructive or soporifically protective, as well as creative. The will-to-believe, therefore, has to be examined and re-examined scrupulously—man being a cunning, rationalizing animal—but that will-to-believe can be ignored or denounced only at the risk of sinking back into mindlessness.

Because of his constant attention to dreams, ultimately it is less important to argue that Albee leans toward the more positive interpretations of *Tiny Alice* than to recognize the implications of the play, itself, as exciting perplex. How it does *not* end is extremely significant. Each member of the audience is compelled to decide (those chronically passive, probably with reluctance) what the next moment after the death/descent of darkness will bring—if indeed there can even be a next moment. *Tiny Alice* is a dramatization of all that must remain tantalizingly beyond the mind's reach: all mysteries whose permanence we deny even as impressions of their persistence accumulate in our experience. The play solicits, proclaims, reveres man's active imagination, its thrust through symbols towards its outermost reaches, its visionary onsets.

In the end, *Tiny Alice*'s mystery is not only unresolved but not even well-defined. Yet, as irresistibly attractive as a black hole with all the blinding consequences of its super density, that mystery is retained. What is knowledge but a holding operation, a beachhead on the immense unknown? A plenitude of possibilities about the nature of the universe and man's miniscule/magisterial parts in it arise from doubt turned back on itself before achieving a dedicated nullity. Can we imagine man's lacking an imagination; can the mind unthink itself?

Tiny Alice is no facile confirmation of faith's efficacy. Even as it celebrates the mind's urgent outreach, the continuous Adamic demand to know the whole truth, it recognizes hazards: the smallness of man adventuring into vastness. The world is full of wonder. A variety of critical responses to his play not only is to be expected by Albee and tolerated; it is, in fact, invited and essential to this theme. Only when the questions end is there reason to worry about the human cause. No phrenological head can accurately map all the compartments of man's intelligence. As a realist of the irrational, Albee knows this—knows that serious literature, like life itself, is a trial embodiment of imagined purpose.

Notes

[1]Edward Albee, "Author's Note" to Tiny Alice (New York: Atheneum, 1965). All further page references appear in the text. For the playwright's comments on Tiny Alice, see the following: Michael E. Rutenberg, "Two Interviews with Edward Albee," contained in Edward Albee: Playwright in Protest (New York: DBS, 1969), pp. 229–60, and Otis L. Guernsey, "Edward Albee Confronts Broadway, 1966," Diplomat, October 1966, pp. 60–63.

[2]Reprints of reviews of the 1965 Billy Rose Theater production of Tiny Alice are reprinted in Harold Clurman, The Divine Pastime: Theatre Essays (New York: Macmillan, 1974), pp. 267–72.

[3]Nation, 18 January 1965.

[4]Anne Paolucci, From Tension to Tonic: The Plays of Edward Albee (Carbondale: Southern Illinois University Press, 1972).

[5]Ruby Cohn, Edward Albee (Minneapolis: The University of Minnesota Press, 1969), p. 28.

[6]Rutenberg, p. 199.

[7]Quoted in Time, 15 January 1965, p. 68.

[8]Mordecai H. Levine, "Albee's Liebstod," College Language Association Journal, 10 (March 1967), pp. 252–55, has demonstrated Albee's use of such "traditional" religious themes and symbolism in The Zoo Story.

⁹For examples of typical critical treatments of these themes, see Daniel Brown, "Albee's Targets," *Satire Newsletter* (Spring 1969):46–52 as well as C. N. Stavrou, "Albee in Wonderland," *Southwest Review* 60 (Winter 1975):46–61.

¹⁰*Time*, 15 January 1965, p. 68.

¹¹We are reminded also that Albee's 1963 play was called, in Czechoslovakia, *Who's Afraid of Franz Kafka?*

¹²The mothering lady from Dubuque and her marital companion have typically been interpreted as angels of death. Citing Elisabeth Kübler-Ross, Albee himself prefers to think of them as figures of a reality *summoned* out of a need for compassion and companionship rather than one *sent*. *New York Times*, 27 January 1980, Section 2, p. 5.

Ritual and Initiation in
The Zoo Story

Mary Castiglie Anderson

ALTHOUGH VARIOUSLY EXPLAINED as a sociopolitical tract, a pessimistic analysis of human alienation, a modern Christian allegory of salvation, and an example of absurdist and nihilist theater, Albee's *The Zoo Story* has managed to absorb these perspectives without exhausting its many levels of meaning with the result that much of the critical controversy which has surrounded the play since its American premier in January 1960 has remained unresolved.[1] However, Albee himself provides what is possibly the best framework for understanding his first play when he speaks of his attempt to depict through his drama the danger of a life lived without "the cleansing consciousness of death."[2] Thus, *The Zoo Story* might well be seen as a portrayal of a ritual confrontation with death and alienation in which Jerry acts the role of shaman/guide who directs the uninitiated Peter through the initiatory rite necessary for Peter to achieve his maturity and autonomy.

Such rituals are, of course, associated with the entering into adulthood and the leaving behind of childish ways. Peter's lack of development and, hence, his need for initiation are immediately apparent in several ways. He is, for instance, relatively inarticulate and unassertive. He tells Jerry, "I'm normally ... reticent" and "I don't express myself too well, sometimes."[3] His responses, when he does give them, tend to be formulaic, showing him to be for the most part a rather unthinking spokesman for the unexamined attitudes of his social class. In his parroting of these values and attitudes, Peter demonstrates the passive acceptance of a child rather than the independence of thought which should characterize an adult. In contrast, the much more linguistically flexible Jerry consistently finds occasion to mock not only Peter's thoughts but the awkwardness and rigidity with which they are expressed. Thus, to Peter's admission of his own feelings of paternal inadequacy because "... naturally, every man wants a son" (p. 16), Jerry employs the cliché, "But that's the way the cookie crumbles." Jerry, whom the stage directions describe here as "lightly mocking," has as his purpose not an attack on Peter's virility or ability to "produce" sons, but rather a mocking challenge of Peter's unquestioning ("naturally") belief in the myths of that virility as well as the emotionless and thoughtless manner of its expression. Similarly, the interchange which is generated through Peter's citation of *Time* magazine reveals the great extent to which Peter's thought is derivative. Peter, himself, self-consciously jokes, "I'm in publishing, not writing" (p. 20). Infant-like, in that he has no real language of his own, Peter has no way of articulating his personal feelings and sensibilities, and without that ability, Peter, it may be argued, lacks any real identity or place within his world. What Jerry effects within the play is the initiation of Peter into an adult world of feelings and the responsibilities which are attendant with their expression.

Jerry sums up Peter's character in one line: "You're a very sweet man and you're possessed of a truly enviable innocence" (p. 23). Peter maintains this innocence by remaining almost completely passive to two forces he has subliminally set up as displaced "parent" figures. Because Peter has invested these figures with such enormous power over the course of his life, they have become for him deterministic structures with seemingly independent lives of their own. The first, his wife, presides over the domestic realm; as a maternal symbol whose individual characteristics remain significantly vague, she seems to exert an influence on Peter which corresponds to the maternal paraphernalia he uses to define himself. The second of these "parental" forces, the essentially male defined and controlled social structure, is the patriarchal authority to which Peter remains obedient. One has, of course, already witnessed Peter's adherence to this authority in the form of his "natural" desire for a son.

Because of his adherence to the forms of that authority, much has been said of Peter as the Organization Man.[4] However, the emphasis has usually been placed on his moral blindness and guilt, which critics have seen as represented by the glasses he cleans and puts on at the opening of the play. Like most of Albee's symbols, the glasses cannot

be limited to a single meaning. Peter is certainly blind to the real world, but he is also an "onlooker" to life in general and to his own life in particular. The price he pays for the protection of his social place (his "cage" according to the metaphor Albee employs) is his identity which, already severely dwarfed, is at the point of being completely obliter- ?
ated. He is, consequently, in a serious personal crisis; his glasses also ·
imply, therefore, that he is searching for something.

    Hints of Peter's dissatisfaction with his own life become apparent as soon as Jerry begins his interrogation/conversation. Within the play, Peter's bench quickly becomes the focal point of the complex web of contradictory desires and fears, intentions and obsessions competing beneath the character's surface rationalizations. When threatened with the loss of the bench late in the play, Peter desperately attempts to articulate the value which the bench has come to have for him: "I sit on this bench almost every Sunday afternoon, in good weather. It's secluded here; there's never anyone sitting here, so I have it all to myself" *bench* (p. 41). He cannot, as yet, consciously appreciate that his weekly sojourn in the park is a small but symbolically significant gesture violating the role of group man. This is the one way Peter has devised to detach himself from the larger group.

    Once outside the parameters of his socioeconomic class, however, Peter risks isolation (immediately suggested by the image of a man sitting alone at a bench in the middle of a large city) by calling attention to himself (becoming "obtrusive") and being approached by someone outside his usual milieu. Because Peter recoils from these risks, the bench symbolizes *both* his desire for autonomy and the crutch he clings to in his effort to go just so far but no further. Peter has been coming to his bench, as he says, "for years" (p. 45), years in which he has maintained his habit as a compromise between freedom and security. Much later in the play, after he has narrated his experience with the dog, Jerry describes the type of emotional sterility, perhaps even death, which results from this kind of reasonable, decorous compromise. In speaking of his renewed relationship with the dog, Jerry says, "And what has been the result: the dog and I have attained a compromise, more of a bargain, really. We neither love nor hurt because we do not *dog* try to reach each other" (p. 36). The commentary applies as well to Peter's lifetime avoidance of pain and risk, an attitude which Jerry challenges by forcing Peter to violate the carefully laid down limits of decorum with which he has circumscribed himself. The action of *The Zoo Story* is, consequently, Peter's rite of exorcism: chaotic, disorienting, generally disruptive in nature, meant to sever his dependencies and to return to Peter the individual's control over his own life which is traditionally practiced by adult members of society. In it, Albee provides a model of a process offering the possibility for meaningful existence in the modern world, a process in which pain is not only unavoidable but is, in the end, regenerative.

In his capacity as shaman of this rite, Jerry, significantly orphaned and socially outcast, appears to Peter as the "Other," or double —the embodiment of characteristics Peter has designated as antithetical to himself. The physical differences between the characters immediately and visually define them as polar and complementary. Peter, although "moving into middle age," dresses and acts in such a way as to "suggest a man younger," while Jerry, though actually younger, has fallen from physical grace and has a "great weariness" suggesting age (p. 11). Peter in his innocence and Jerry in his "over-sanity" (Albee's term) both lack completeness; each provides the other with a "missing half." Robert Bennett has pointed out that, though most critics see the pair as polar opposites, "Jerry approaches Peter. . . . as an enlightened brother."[5] Actually, both evaluations are true. As is the case with doubles, the characters are irrevocably linked *and* set apart by means of their antithetical characteristics.

The double in literature tends to emerge in the consciousness of the first self (in this case, Peter) at the moment of crisis for the purpose of effecting some major change.[6] C. G. Jung's terminology for this second self—"the immortal within the mortal man" and "the long expected friend of the soul"[7]—interestingly echoes Jerry's intimation that, on at least some level, his arrival was not completely expected:

Jerry: Peter, do I annoy you, or confuse you?

Peter: (*lightly*) Well, I must confess that this wasn't the kind of afternoon I'd anticipated.

Jerry: You mean I wasn't the gentleman you were expecting.

Peter: I wasn't expecting anybody.

Jerry: No, I don't imagine you were. But I'm here, and I'm not leaving (pp. 37–38).

Ultimately, the appearance of such doubles presupposes the presence, both in the individual and the society which he represents, of a natural psychic equilibrium which of necessity attempts to reassert itself. Whether consciously or unconsciously summoned, Jerry responds to

Peter's subliminal attraction to individually, a-rationality, and rebellion by playing "dark twin" to Peter's "favored son." Since Peter's personal identity is at stake, Jerry is a call for renewal generated by Peter's own psyche. This explains why Peter does not leave, although he is clearly annoyed by Jerry's presence. Peter's summoning of Jerry is also seen in the hints of Jerry's own lack of free will in shaping the events which take place during their encounter.

In his dealings with Peter, Jerry seems to be following a format with an outcome so inevitable that it may be prophesied almost as soon as he encounters Peter: "You'll read about it in the papers tomorrow, if you don't see it on your T.V. tonight" (p. 15). Jerry's plan seems less the product of his own invention than the result of some other-worldly revelation. Although, from the outset, Jerry appears to have an inchoate understanding of the inevitability of his meeting with Peter, it is not until these inevitabilities have played themselves out that he is able to acknowledge his complicity with them: "I think that while I was at the zoo I decided that I would walk north ... northerly rather ... until I found you ... or somebody ... and I decided that I would talk to you ... I would tell you things ... and the things that I would tell you would ... well, here we are. You see? Here we *are*. But ... I don't know ... could I have planned all this? No ... no, I couldn't have. But I think I did ... and now you'll know what you'll see in your T.V." (p. 48). None of this is meant to suggest that Jerry is simply a volitionless symbol. On the contrary, as the above speech suggests, he is a fully dimensional character with complex motivations of his own. Yet Albee, at his best, can masterfully create characters who are both surrealistically dreamlike and perfectly realistic. In this play, Peter and Jerry reveal different aspects of one personality *and* represent very real people in a very real situation. Peter's reactions to Jerry both correspond to struggles within himself and are realistic responses to the situation which Jerry creates.

By creating the situation, or argument, over the bench, Jerry forces Peter to acknowledge the existence of his other half, so that what has been a continuous monologue for Jerry at last becomes a clearly polarized debate, the prerequisite for resolution. As the archetypal "stranger," Jerry intrudes on Peter's solitude, his personal affairs and, most importantly, his bench. In doing so, Jerry forces Peter to consider the value which he has invested in his personal symbol. In the face of Jerry's challenge for proprietorship of the bench, Peter's dilemma becomes increasingly difficult. If on the one hand he cedes the bench to Jerry without putting up any sort of struggle, Peter will be renouncing his one claim to personal distinction and succumb completely to his stereotypic role of child-like passivity. On the other hand, confrontation with Jerry will force him to acknowledge both the reality of his own will and the existence of a contradictory reality threatening to his identification with a collective structure. Jerry, priest and playwright, orchestrates the ritual/drama between them in order to externalize Peter's internal conflict and force a choice on Peter's part. Choice implies personal responsibility, which is the hallmark of the initiated adult. For his own part, Jerry, in presiding over the rite through which Peter enters the world of the initiated, goes on to gain an identity or definition of himself. He is shaman or guide in the initiatory rites, and, indeed, Jerry consistently acts as though he were the keeper of mystical secrets which he can only just share with his unenlightened counterpart.

Much of the stage action in *The Zoo Story* does bear the mark of ritual. And while there is an implicit connection between all drama and ritual, Albee seems to call special attention to this connection within *The Zoo Story*. Jerry's actions when he catalogues his possessions and when he relates the parable of the dog "as if reading from a billboard" (p. 30), ending with an incantation that is a kind of litany and invocation, are explicitly ritualistic. Throughout the play, Jerry also employs Biblical language, combining it with a speech pattern so vernacular that the juxtaposition emphasizes a dichotomy between sacred and profane, the spiritual and the temporal—a dichotomy which Jerry will eventually resolve. The ritualistic quality of the play is also conveyed through its setting—"a place apart" (p. 11)—where, should Peter yell, no one would hear him—and in Albee's suggestion of how Jerry should use space on stage: "The following long speech, it seems to me, should be done with a great deal of action, to achieve a hypnotic effect on Peter, and on the audience, too" (p. 29). Accordingly, Jerry tends to direct his own actions during his long monologue as if following a dance or ritualistic scheme: "I'll start walking around in a little while, and eventually I'll sit down" (p. 19).[8]

The key element of Jerry's ritual, the story of himself and the dog, contains all of the elements that have long been recognized as parts of the mythic quest. The hero, Jerry, must gain admittance to a certain place which has associations with the underworld. He is prevented first by an old crone (his landlady). Once he gets past her by repeating the right formula, he is accosted by a "raging beast" (the dog) which he must either tame or kill. Having undergone these ordeals, he can resume his place in the real or everyday world with the possession of some new knowledge and understanding. Significantly, Jerry defines this as "something to do with how sometimes it's necessary to go a long distance out of the way in order to come back a short distance correctly" (p. 21).

Moreover, the mythic aspects of Jerry's tale are brought into high relief by the fact that the rooming house clearly has symbolic associations with the underworld; it is a place full of obvious outcasts, people somehow "dead" to most of society, as Peter admits: "It's so... unthinkable. I find it hard to believe that people such as that really *are*" (p. 28). This underworld is, in turn, connected to the unconscious. Jerry's rooming house in Albee's first play functions much like Miss Alice's house does in *Tiny Alice*—as a dream-like center of mystery. As with Miss Alice's house, it is a place with many rooms and levels, having four stories. Jerry lives on the top floor, the place closest to consciousness. The rooms are all "laughably small," separate from each other, and "better as you go down, floor by floor" into unknown territory (p. 22). Jerry carefully points out that he does not know "any of the people on the third and second floors" (p. 27). As he says of one of the unknown rooms, "there's somebody lives there, but I don't know who it is. I've never seen who it is. Never, never ever" (p. 22).

Significantly, within primitive rites of initiation, the novice is often led into a house representing a microcosm of society or of human consciousness. The initiate's entrance into such a house is his symbolic installation at the center of the universe. Anthropologist Arnold Van Gennep in *Rites of Passage* defines the first step in this type of initiation as the rite of separation.[9] Typically, the hero must encounter the labyrinth separating him from his former life. The entrance into new life is symbolized as passing through a door, since to cross a threshold is to unite oneself with a new world. Thus, Jerry draws specific attention to his place of confrontation with the dog: "And where better, where better to communicate one single, simple-minded idea than in an *entrance hall?* Where? It would be a START! Where better to *make a beginning* ... to understand and just possibly be understood" (italics added) (p. 35).

The landlady and her dog are guardians of the threshold, and, as in the traditional quest format, they must be honored and appeased. The former, a displaced sybil-figure, personifies the seductress and the witch. Jerry describes her as a "fat, ugly, mean, stupid, unwashed, misanthropic, cheap, drunken bag of garbage" who comes after him with her "sweaty lust" (p. 28). Usually this figure tries to prevent the seeker's entrance into the place which is the source of knowledge. If the person has the right information — such as the knowledge of the

labyrinth design, the right password, or if he makes the right request—
he finds his road easily. If not, the woman devours him.[10] Jerry, however, has found the formula to undercut her power: "But I have found
a way to keep her off. When she presses herself to my body and
mumbles about her room and how I should come there, I merely
say: but, Love; wasn't yesterday enough for you, and the day before?"
(p. 28).

The Yet Jerry, as questing hero, must also find a way to avoid the
dog who functions as an avatar of the monstrous landlady when she,
herself, is not present. To be sure, the dog is an extension of the
landlady; in fact, they look alike: "She had forgotten her bewildered
lust, and her eyes were wide open for the first time. They looked like
the dog's eyes" (p. 32). Traditionally, dogs have been associated in
mythology with the priesthood of Great Mother figures and the "Male
votaries of the Great Goddess who prostituted themselves in her
name."[11] Like its owner, the dog in *The Zoo Story* is bent on devouring
Jerry: "this dog wasn't indifferent. From the very beginning he'd snarl
and then go for me, to get one of my legs. Not like he was rabid you
know; he was sort of a stumbly dog, but he wasn't half-assed either. It
was a good stumbly run; but I always got away … *(Puzzles)* I still don't
know to this day how the other roomers manage it, but you know what I
think: I think it had to do only with me" (p. 30), and like its owner, it can
only be appeased with a symbolic offering. Jerry, as we learn, makes an
effort to appease the dog by offering it various pieces of food with
pretended good will. In the cases of both the landlady and her pet, the
offering is a fiction, pretended sexual encounters and pretended good
will, which is designed to act as a symbolic substitute for the sacrifice of
Jerry. In each case, the fiction is created in order to prevent the
rendering of the desired object which is, literally, Jerry's flesh. Yet such
sacrifices or substitutions ultimately prove to be unsatisfactory. Jerry, in
his desperation, attempts to do away with the canine sentry who blocks
his free entry into the rooming house by placing poison in one of the
"offerings" which he makes to the dog which he calls "a descendant of
the puppy that guarded the gates of hell or some such resort" (p. 33).

The result of this act is to place Jerry in the next stage of the
initiatory process. In the format of primitive rites of initiation, the
ordeal for the novice typically has four basic stages which lead to his
rebirth as a new, mature individual: separation from his mother and
from his counterparts, confrontation with danger and death, hallucination or loss of consciousness with a resultant identification with the
external world, and, finally, an inevitable sense of loss upon the return

to the world of ordinary consciousness. As we have already seen, Jerry is set apart by both the landlady and her dog and has been locked in a desperate struggle to avoid being consumed or subsumed by his adversaries. The essence of Jerry's struggle has been the preservation of his pre-initiatory identity. However, with the events following the poisoning and recovery of the dog, both Jerry and the dog are transformed by a seeming merging of their separate consciousnesses and the creation of a new knowledge or understanding between them. The possibility of the dog's recovery creates in Jerry the expectation of a transformation: "I wanted the dog to live so that I could see what our new relationship might come to" (p. 33).

That new relationship is shaped by Jerry's loss of self-consciousness and the subsequent momentary communion which he and the dog achieve: "during that twenty seconds or two hours that we looked into each other's faces, we made contact" (p. 34). The transformation is poignant and personal for Jerry, arousing within him a previously unfelt need for a sense of kinship with the external world. In the encounter, the two become each other. That such communion is possible is the essence of Jerry's revelation.

Yet Jerry also learns that, as a sentient being, he is subject to more than biological needs and impulses which are necessary for physical survival. The understanding — his revelation — immediately alienates him from nature by virtue of his rationality, self-reflection, and ability to define his experience. He simultaneously realizes both the separateness of personal enlightenment and the longing for companionship which such a sense of separateness engenders. Such transcendence is, then, not achieved without cost. There is the separation from those who are uninitiated and have therefore not shared the experience. There is the sense of loss of the transcendental when the initiate returns to ordinary, albeit made-over, consciousness. Thus, despite the validity and intensity of their transcendent experience, Jerry and the dog must eventually re-enter the world of time and space and face the inevitable sense of loss which accompanies all such returns. The two are no longer "one," and yet they cannot simply return to their old relationship of two set against each other. They surrender to a new "fiction" in order to define their made-over relationship: "When the dog and I see each other, we both stop where we are. We regard each other with a mixture of sadness and suspicion, and then we feign indifference. We walk past each other safely; we have an understanding. It's very sad, but you have to admit it's an understanding" (p. 35).

While Jerry clearly speaks for Albee in regard to the necessity of such fictions or understandings in the face of the "sadness and suspicion" of return to the non-transcendental, that need has long been recognized as an important after-effect of the experience of initiation. Ortega y Gasset, for instance, writes: "In the vacuum arising after he has left behind animal life, [Man] devotes himself to a series of non-biological occupations which are not imposed by nature but invented by himself. This invented life—invented as a novel or a play is invented —man calls human life, well being. It is not given to man as its fall is given to a stone or the stock of its organic acts—eating, flying, nesting— to an animal. He makes it himself, beginning by inventing it."[12]

It is this vacuum which is the source of man's creative life, and while Jerry has long been seen as Albee's symbol for the modern artist, what has not been fully understood is that the source of Jerry's creative drive is the sense of loss created by his own initiatory experience and related in his tale of himself and the dog. Art, then, is born of both vision and suffering, out of both gain and loss: "I have learned that neither kindness nor cruelty by themselves, independent of each other creates any effect beyond themselves; and I have learned that the two combined together, at the same time, are the teaching emotion. And what is gained is loss" (p. 36).

Jerry's lines suggest that, as long as those impulses are kept rigidly apart, they cannot convey the totality of human experience. This enforced separation, in turn, precludes any movement beyond these emotions to stronger expressions of love and hate. However, society, implicitly equated with the zoo within Albee's play, tends to separate human emotions and impulses into appropriate categories or "cages." In extreme cases, such as that of Peter, the result of such careful isolation of emotions is a lack of identity or completeness of self.

Conflicting emotions, such as the kindness and cruelty of which Jerry spoke, simultaneously function in the full complexity of human motives, and no complete self-understanding is possible unless individuals acknowledge their often simultaneous capacity for good and evil. While Jerry's experience with the dog has brought him a greater knowledge of the facts of his existence, it has also caused him to lose the purity of simple, clearly defined motives in an easily apprehended and described universe. It is the paradoxical complexity of that universe which often leads man to create fictions as a means of survival. In the end, all explanations become mere fictions because of the inadequacy of language in the face of such complexity. This awareness on

Jerry's part accounts for his paradoxical use and condemnation of such verbal fictions as well as the extreme self-consciousness of his language.[13]

Jerry goes further in his analysis of the inadequacy of language to express the totality of experience: "And *was* trying to feed the dog an act of love? And, perhaps, was the dog's attempt to bite me *not* an act of love? If we can so misunderstand, well then, why have we invented the word love in the first place?" (p. 36). Words in *The Zoo Story*, as this passage indicates, are another example of a "cage" imposed upon reality. Jerry here attempts to find the category, or pigeonhole, that will help him understand and order his experience with the dog. At the same time, however, he resists all categories, which he perceives as limiting and therefore falsifying experience. Any definition, he implies, would exclude some aspect of the whole experience.

The problem of setting limits which surfaces in Jerry's consideration of the delimiting nature of language is also apparent in Jerry's constantly voiced concern with the issue of circumscription, both voluntary and involuntary, as Jerry moves from a consideration of the separation of humans from animals, to that of humans from humans, and ultimately to the individual from awareness of himself. To understand how he perceives these divisions, one must look to the numerous references he makes throughout the play to the separation between animals and humans. He went to the zoo, he says, to see about "the way people exist with animals and animals with each other and with people" (p. 39). Early in the play, he focuses on the separation of Peter's parakeets from their natural predators, the cats. When he finally begins to relate the story about the zoo, he gets as far as the lion keeper entering the lion's cage before he begins to "enter" Peter's "cage" by challenging him for the bench. Jerry's own encounter is with an animal who, at first, responds to him simply as one animal would respond to another in nature; that is, without acknowledging the "understanding" of "one's place" imposed by civilization. Jerry eventually realizes that it was this level of understanding which provided common ground between them. He attempts to rediscover this common ground with Peter as a basis for their communication.

To establish such a common ground with Peter, Jerry resorts to the threat of violence. When he begins to punch and insult Peter, Jerry moves them toward an interchangeability that reinforces their relationship as doubles whose very opposition presupposes their unity. That is, the confrontation Jerry initiates over the bench isolates and focuses the sharp yet arbitrary differences between Peter and Jerry which, when broken down by means of their mutual anger, reveal their essential sameness.[14]

Jerry's expressed need for Peter's bench is an incidental focus for his real need to possess Peter's being, or, in his own words, to "get through to" the other man, to "make contact" (p. 34). Jerry's choice of the bench is obvious since Peter identifies that particular object with himself. Once Peter is threatened with its loss, he articulates the identification by associating it with his adulthood, his manhood, and his sense of responsibility: "I've come here for years; I have hours of great pleasure, great satisfaction, right here. And that's important to a man. I'm a responsible person, and I'm a GROWNUP. This is my bench and you have no right to take it from me" (p. 45).

In challenging Peter's right to the bench, Jerry leads Peter away from the social structures dividing them—structures which make Peter unable to accept the original brotherhood Jerry offers—by provoking him to a level of interaction at which they can share experience, that level outside society which Jerry calls "animal." Their conflict first clearly differentiates them as antagonists and then dissolves the differences by creating for each a reflection of his own antagonism in the other. In the end, the sameness of the mutual violence comes to overshadow the differences which originally gave rise to their violent impulses. Thus, when Jerry rushes to grab Peter by the collar, Albee's stage directions indicate that their faces must almost touch (p. 46).

Within *The Zoo Story*, the unity and reciprocity which violence effects finds its most striking expression in the climactic tableau scene (p. 47). There, for all their initial differences, Peter and Jerry unite beyond all definitions, structures, and language—even the line between victim and victimizer becomes blurred, as it was earlier in the case of Jerry and the dog. The moment of their transcendence of these fictions is necessarily one of silence and absence of movement. In that moment, too, the act leading to Jerry's death loses its distinction as either suicide or murder. Jerry's sacrifice/death is, then, necessary: the cultural crisis culminating in the characters' violent interaction over the bench must find an outlet upon which to expend itself; otherwise their distinctions (and, by extension, the social order) cannot be restored.

The lesson inherent in Peter's initiation is, consistent with the motif of the double, just the reverse of Jerry's, since Peter has been all but subsumed by human-defined culture from which he must eventually be severed by reawakening his less reflective impulses. Jerry as much as predicts this early in the play when he tells Peter that he "looks like an animal man" (p. 18). When Peter finally "loses control," he undergoes a series of basic emotions, he becomes "tearful," "beside himself," "hysterical" with laughter, "whining," "enraged." For the first time in the play (and, one might conjecture, for the first time in his adult life), Peter's responses are immediate reactions to real feelings, uninterrupted by the lag of self-conscious deliberation.

The direct alignment of "animal" and "rational" within Peter fulfills the intention of Jerry's ritual. Ritualistic overtones continue in the chant Peter whispers as Jerry is dying. According to the stage directions, Peter repeats "Oh my God, oh my God, oh my God," "many times, very rapidly" before he breaks down in tears and exits, uttering the same words in "a pitiful howl" (p. 49). The cry, echoing Jerry's scream of "an infuriated and fatally wounded animal" when he impales himself on the knife, must certainly be meant to be one of recognition. Albee's drama, unlike many of its contemporaries, is nothing if not cathartic.

There has been a tendency to interpret the ending of *The Zoo Story* as Albee's parody of religious feeling. On the contrary, Peter's ritual, in which he sits on a bench reading a book every Sunday "in good weather," is the playwright's example of the ritualistic impulse grown remote from its original roots and compromised by the pervasive influence of materialism. Though still alive, the impulse has, to use Jerry's terminology, "no effect beyond itself."[15] Unlike the modern mentality, the pre-civilized mind, as it is reflected in original initiation ceremonies, views the frightening agents of the rite itself and the often violent symbolic death the initiate must face as regenerative, causing the novice to move from innocence to experience. The initiate is separated from a narcissistic attachment to his mother and, by means of his experience with death, becomes an adult member of his tribe. Albee's play employs a similar structure, and perhaps it is on this basis that it is often misunderstood. However, unlike primitive initiation, Albee's ritual of initiation is not an initiation into society but, instead, into autonomy, into the maturity to resist surrender to absolute systems of belief and external sources of self-definition. Peter's break with the security of the social collective is symbolized by the severance from his bench and by the confrontation he has with death. When Jerry takes out and clicks open an "ugly looking knife," the realization of his mortality and the apparently arbitrary imperatives that exist beyond rationality dawn on Peter: "You *are* mad! You're stark raving mad. YOU'RE GOING TO KILL ME!" (p. 46). Jerry, by his death, incorporates the principle he represents back into society, an idea amplified by his contention that Peter will see Jerry's face on television—the reflector of modern America's experiences and self-images. His death also restores order, not cyclically, but with the crucial difference implied that Peter must restructure his life without his bench from which, as Jerry tells him, he has been "dispossessed" (p. 49).

The message of *The Zoo Story*, as of later Albee plays, is that the patterns inherited in life are of necessity untested. Yet, in reaching beyond such patterns, Jerry and Peter come to what Lawyer in *Tiny Alice* calls "the edge of the abyss" to face the primal fears of abandonment and loss of identity. Put another way, the characters temporarily escape all limits, dissolve all distinctions, encounter formlessness, and, if the form of their initiation holds true, strike their own bargain with reality and experience. Inherent in the structure of Albee's play is the idea that all patterns are created fictions, fictions which are necessary nonetheless, since they are the only means through which experience can be made comprehensible. Yet, because humans create their fictions, they can both control and change them. Albee holds forth the possibility, through Peter, that the disintegration of an old identity (an identity "borrowed" from identification with external authority) along with the inevitable panic such disintegration encourages may be the means for a new, more consciously formed personality. Such life-shaping structures, his play suggests, must be created rather than inherited by the individual and must continuously be reformed, so as never to be mistaken for the absolute and implacable.

Notes

[1]See, for instance, Michael E. Rutenberg, *Edward Albee: Playwright in Protest* (New York: Avon Books, 1969), p. 29; Mary M. Nilan, "Albee's *The Zoo Story:* Alienated Man and the Nature of Love, *Modern Drama* 16 (June 1973):58–59; Rose A. Zimbardo, "Symbolism and Naturalism in Edward Albee's *The Zoo Story*," *Twentieth Century Literature* 8 (April 1962):15; Gilbert Debusscher, *Edward Albee —Tradition and Renewal*, trans. Anne D. Williams (Brussels: American Studies Center 1967), p. 12; Anne Paulocci, *From Tension to Tonic: The Plays of Edward Albee* (Carbondale: Southern Illinois University Press, 1972), p. 43. For critical analyses focusing on the questions the play poses rather than the solutions it offers, see Ruby Cohn, *Edward Albee* (Minneapolis: University of Minnesota

Press, 1969), p. 10; C. W. E. Bigsby, *Albee* (Edinburgh: Oliver and Boyd, 1969), p. 16; Robert Bennett, "Tragic Vision in *The Zoo Story*," *Modern Drama* 20 (March, 1977):58.

[2] Introduction to Edward Albee, *The Plays*, Volume I (New York: Coward, McCann & Geoghegan, 1981), p. 10.

[3] Edward Albee, *The American Dream* and *The Zoo Story* (New York: Signet, 1963), p. 19 and p. 20. All subsequent page references appear in the text.

[4] Rutenberg, p. 30.

[5] Bennett, p. 60.

[6] For a comprehensive analysis of the double in literature see Carl F. Keppler, *The Literature of the Second Self* (Tucson: University of Arizona Press, 1972).

[7] C. G. Jung, *Four Archetypes: Mother/Rebirth/Spirit/Trickster*, trans. R. F. C. Hull (Princeton: Princeton University Press, Bollingen Series, 1959, 1969), p. 55.

[8] Jerry's directorial role is Albee's subtle use of the alienation effect, meant to remind the audience that the stage frames mimetic, not real, action. Albee, in his characterization of Jerry, strikes a balance between realistic and stylized actions, an aesthetic balance that reflects the theme of balancing opposites.

[9] Anold von Gennep, *The Rites of Passage*, trans. Monika B. Vizedom (Chicago: University of Chicago Press, 1960), pp. 65–115; see also Mircea Eliade, *Birth and Rebirth: The Religious Meanings of Initiation in Human Culture*, trans. Willard R. Trask (New York: Harper and Row, 1958), p. x.

[10] Eliade, p. 62.

[11] Erich Neumann, *The Origins and History of Consciousness*, trans. R. F. C. Hull (Princeton: Princeton University Press, Bollingen Series, 1954), p. 61. There have been various other explanations of mythological animals. Joseph Campbell in *The Hero with a Thousand Faces* writes of how the hero "comes at last to the Lord of the Underworld ... [who] rushes against him, horribly bellowing; but if the shaman is sufficiently skillful he can soothe the monster back again with promises of luxurious offerings" (p. 100); Joseph Henderson in *The Wisdom of the Serpent* calls the mystic animals "sacred animals possessing secret wisdom the dreamer wishes to learn" and representatives of the experience of "submission to a power greater than the hero himself" (p. 51). C. G. Jung refers to them as "part of the instinctive psyche" which has been lost or separated from consciousness like a "loss of soul" (Jung, p. 73).

[12] Quoted in Tony Tanner, *City of Words: American Fiction, 1950–1970* (New York: Harper and Row, 1971), p. 29.

[13] Tanner in *City of Words* calls the self-conscious use of language, "foregrounding." In his view this stylistic device permeates most of American literature. His thesis is that American writers particularly have been overwhelmingly concerned with the tension between structure or artifice and reality. Though Tanner does not refer to Albee in his book (which deals only with fiction), his contention that "American writers seem from the first to have felt how tenuous, arbitrary, and even illusory, are the verbal constructs which men call description of reality" applies equally to the playwright. We can see this tension in Jerry's frustration with the inadequacy of definition. See also Robert S. Wallace, "The Zoo Story: Albee's Attack on Fiction," *Modern Drama* 16 (June 1973), pp. 49–54; Arthur K. Oberg, "Edward Albee: His Language and Imagination," *Prairie Schooner* 40 (1966):139–46.

[14]This thesis of the role of violence in ritual and drama is put forth by René Girard, *Violence and the Sacred*, trans. Patrick Gregory (Baltimore: Johns Hopkins University Press, 1977).

[15]Albee's play realizes many of the tenets of Antonin Artaud's "Theatre of Cruelty." Artaud's theory was that theatre would representationally confront modern humans with their most primal impulses in order to annihilate their comforting social forms and reinvolve them in their own lives.

The Pirandello in Albee
The Problem of Knowing in
The Lady from Dubuque

THOMAS P. ADLER

"Reality is too *little* for me."
—*Listening*

I'll make toast; I'll make buttered toast.
That will be heaven. Won't that be
heaven, Oscar?
Well, it will be *toast*.
—*The Lady from Dubuque*

A LTHOUGH EDWARD ALBEE'S *The Lady from Dubuque* was neither a
critical nor a popular success when it opened on Broadway early in
1980 only to close precipitately after twelve performances,[1] Otis
Guernsey, Jr. rightly includes it among *The Best Plays of* 1979–1980,
predicting with some justification, I suspect, that "this distinguished
and durable play ... will surely be heard in time, globally."[2] From one
point of view, *Lady from Dubuque* is a continuation of several stylistic and
thematic and structural themes in Albee's plays. It is related, for example, in its corruscating wit and sometimes bitter exchanges between
hosts and guests to *Who's Afraid of Virginia Woolf?* (1962); in its focus on
the rights and responsibilities of family and friends to *A Delicate Balance*
(1966); and in its form as a death-watch to *All Over* (1971). From yet
another perspective, however, it is a culmination of Albee's interest in

109

epistemological and ontological problems, a strand that can be traced back through *Counting the Ways* and *Listening* (1976), the pair of lengthy one-act plays written immediately preceding it, and to *Tiny Alice* (1964). Even a cursory examination of *Dubuque*'s language reveals Albee's interest in—almost obsession with—the problem of knowing. The word "know" recurs, in fact, again and again in the text as both the play's characters and audience are asked to consider exactly who and what can actually be known — for within the play we are asked if we can, indeed, know ourselves or others, substances or only surfaces, essences or only their representations. Moreover, the play goes on to challenge its audience with questions concerning not only the content of our knowledge but the very process by which we come to know. *Tiny Alice* forces us to question the dependability of knowledge obtained in the most usual fashion, through the reading of observable phenomena, by asking if our merely thinking something makes it so.

The central metaphysical concern of *Tiny Alice* is clearly the problem of finite man's understandable tendency to question the reality of what cannot be perceived by the senses and, following from that, the almost universal human need to concretize the abstract, to discover or — barring that — to create a manageable representation of the unknown. Brother Julian, the play's central figure, finds upsetting and disorienting man's anthropomorphizing habit through which he simplifies mystery in order to control what cannot be understood. The widespread need to "represent" something before it can be worshipped plunges him into a dark night of the soul, for to "personify," to resort to symbolism, is to "limit it, demean it."[3] That anthropomorphizing frame of mind is rendered visually in the stage setting: in the library of the mansion where the action occurs is a model of the mansion, exact in all its details. Perhaps, it is hinted, there is even a miniature model of this model in the library *within* the model! Ultimately, the play moves its audience toward a direct confrontation with the epistemological question of which came first: the model or the mansion? If the mansion, then the model is merely a shadow of a pre-existing form; if the model, then the mansion is only a replica of the model. A similar question can be asked of the characters on stage: are there also miniatures of them in the model? And, if so, is the onstage library simply a room within a larger model, with characters watching these characters watching?

Of those characters, Julian is a priest of the cult of "THE ABSTRACT," which for him is the only "REAL" (p. 188) and True. Yet, paradoxically—and herein lies the crux of his test—he can only finally achieve spiritual union with the abstract Tiny Alice (sonamed perhaps to suggest the very diminishment of the gods he has always rebelled against) by marrying and uniting sexually (again, a descent from the spiritual to the physical) with her surrogate, Miss Alice. So has not Julian, then, ultimately "confuse[d] the representative of a…thing with the thing itself" (p. 39)? As a last, desperate defense against his fear of the Void—against the possibility that not only has he "worship[ped] the symbol and not the substance" (p. 105) but that no substance resides behind the symbol, that "THERE IS NOTHING THERE!" (p. 164)— Julian must, through a tremendous act of faith that is one of the illusions Albee claims all men use to get through life, *will* the presence of Tiny Alice at the point of his death so that his sacrifice on her altar will not have been in vain. In this most philosophically Absurd of Albee's plays, he asks: How many dimensions of multi-layered reality are real, and how many simply a figment of man's imaginings? Finally, maybe only the mouse in the model or the wig-adorned phrenological head (which diagrams man's organs of knowing) can be worshipped. But the unsettling possibility remains that those, too, have no objective existence.

Counting the Ways likewise hinges on the distinction between "knowing" as a certainty and only "thinking" that something is so as a supposition. What is at question here, though, is not metaphysical truth, but the truth of the emotions. Each desiring from the other an auricular assurance and measurement, the man and the woman (called simply "He" and "She") ask of each other, "Do you love me?"[4] But to quantify what is essentially qualitative, to measure depth of feelings by words is, as Lear learned too late, to reduce. In *The Lady from Dubuque*, it will be the pain of dying and loss that cannot be measured, and because of its futility, such attempts at measuring the unmeasurable inevitably become little more than childish games.[5] Within *Counting the Ways*, such Lear-like attempts to measure love inevitably result in games such as "She loves me? She loves me not?" or "Me loves he? Not me loves he?"— the latter while putting the petals back on—(pp. 13, 17). In the end, such games are so obviously incapable of proving that one loves or is loved that the lovers are ultimately left to live on faith in the same way that Julian dies on faith. But in this "Vaudeville," the question of knowing extends as well to the actors' and audience's awareness and perception of themselves. When a "sign descends" and lights up commanding, "IDENTIFY YOURSELVES" (p. 35), the actors step out of their roles as characters, address the audience now as actors (as they earlier had as characters) and improvise a thumbnail sketch of themselves, sending the audience to consult their programs *after* the play" (p. 36) if they desire more information about the real lives of the actor and actress playing He and She. But to what extent can that sketch or the printed biography consisting of external facts and figures really define the person? And when the sign descends, the members of the audience might have the uneasy feeling at first that *they* are each being required to identify themselves to the others sitting around them.

If *Tiny Alice* asks about knowing religious truth and *Counting the Ways* about ascertaining truths of the heart, *Listening* explores one's ability to know and, thus, to control the psyche of another person. In this Strindbergian "Chamber Play," The Woman, whom we take to be an analyst in a psychiatric hospital, can manipulate and ultimately drive the patient/inmate Girl to suicide. The Woman is literal-minded, cold, emotionless, rational—so calculating that her extreme rationality becomes a kind of Iago-like rationalism devoid of moral scruple or consideration. By knowing the way in which The Girl's mind works, The Woman is able to prompt The Girl to use the sharp glass in the empty fountain to slit her own wrists. Able to perceive "the movement, when an idea happens," The Woman tells The Girl, "I can hear your pupils widen" (pp. 74, 77). Playing on The Girl's fear of blood (menstruation) by graphically describing the analogous case history of another female patient, The Woman will drive the girl to suicide just as surely as The Woman has already driven The Man to tears by turning away from and rejecting him in a previous encounter since, as The Man points out, "Effect comes *after* act" (p. 131). The full force of The Woman's diabolical power of suggestion is seen in the Hedda-like line, "Done beautifully" (p. 152), as The Girl holds up her bleeding wrists. So The Woman has indeed been "listening" all along to the signals the psychotic Girl has been sending out.

This consistent concern on the part of the playwright with what and how people can know—or hope to know—in the metaphysical, emotional, and psychic spheres in all of these works suggests Albee's position about reality as multi-layered and essentially unknowable in any but a relativistic sense — one of the hallmarks of Pirandello's thought as well. Moreover, these brief remarks perhaps disclose other hints of Pirandello's recurrent emphases: on the fragmentation and multiplicity of personality; on the convergence and/or contrast between life and theater, role-playing and reality, the mask and its wearer; and on the audience's self-reflexivity. And in light of these themes, *The Lady from Dubuque*, which insists on the necessity to perceive life as essentially multi-leveled, seems to be Albee's most Pirandellian play to date.[6]

Clearly, the most obviously Pirandellian aspect of *The Lady from Dubuque* is the audience's awareness that they are watching a play—an awareness pursued thematically by Pirandello in such works as *Six Characters in Search of an Author* and *Tonight We Improvise,* which are aesthetic inquiries into the nature of the theatre—extends to *The Lady from Dubuque,* wherein Albee exploits this Modernist convention of making the audience conscious of themselves *as* audience by having the characters address them directly in either brief remarks or longer speeches some eighty or so times. As his "Performance Note" indicates, "this is done without self-consciousness, quite openly, and without interrupting the flow of the play."[7] As with much of *The Lady from Dubuque,* the device does not depart from Albee's earlier practice, extending back through *Counting the Ways* (where, as we have noticed, the technique is employed adroitly and purposefully), *Box* and *Quotations from Chairman Mao Tse-Tung* (1968), *The American Dream* (1961), and even *The Sandbox* (1960). In *The American Dream,* Grandma, the most realistically conceived among characters who are deliberately drawn as cartoon figures, steps out of her role and stands back from the action to comment upon it, becoming, in a sense, a member of the audience. Similarly, *The Sandbox* is the first instance in Albee in which Pirandellian motifs — illusion/reality, play-acting, life/art — become a concern, as well as the first to employ characters as symbol, myth, and archetype.

To be sure, the self-conscious, Pirandellian lines which the characters in *The Lady from Dubuque* speak directly to the audience serve several functions. Sometimes, they simply furnish exposition; at other times, they provide the kind of editorializing to underscore a point that we ordinarily expect from a choral character. Infrequently, they are philosophic or nostalgic or sardonic meditations on some facet of existence. Often, their tone is defensive or mildly conspiratorial, demanding some complicity from the audience in the form of a supportive or empathic response in the face of a challenge issuing from one of the other characters. No matter what their purpose, however, Albee insists emphatically that in every instance these lines be spoken not by the actors as actors (as had been the case in *Counting the Ways*), but instead by the actors *in* character. As his stage directions indicate, "It is of the utmost importance that the actors make it clear that it is not they, but the characters, who are aware of the presence of the audience" (p. ix). Furthermore, these lines are not in the nature of "asides" as traditionally understood in drama, since the other onstage characters hear them and respond to them as they normally would to dialogue exchanges. Indeed, many of these lines are addressed simultaneously to the other characters and across the footlights to the audience. So while this technique is non-illusionistic—deliberately heightening our awareness that we are in a theatre watching a play—this device ultimately requires not so much that we reflect on ourselves as an audience but rather that we regard ourselves as, and associate ourselves with, the onstage characters who represent us. We are among the guests at this party-turned-deathwatch. Instead of being mere observers, we—though silent—are participants in this ritual. Here, then, Albee shifts emphasis from audience as audience to audience as character.

In regard to *The Lady from Dubuque,* the action which the audience is expected both to bear witness to and take a part in might well be termed a "coming of death" play, with Elizabeth, *The Lady from Dubuque,* and her black companion Oscar as the summoners; yet the drama is radically different from the medieval morality plays in theme and tone, since it reveals no specifically religious orientation. Nor does it end with any assurance of salvation in an afterlife. And, too, the play focuses much less on the dying person than it does on the survivor, thus linking it closely to *All Over.* Jo, dying of an unspecified disease which has all the symptoms of cancer, vents her pain and bitterness on the friends who gather around, "need[ing] a surface to bounce it all off of" (p. 47). Knowing that she must not succumb to self-pity, that if she cries for herself she might fall totally apart, she requires also a husband who possesses the necessary strength to see her through her last agony—as she becomes less and less, as she finally joins "The very dead; who hear nothing; who remember nothing; who are nothing" (p. 138). Her husband Sam, however, also knows his needs, especially the necessity to "hold on to the object we're losing" and not let go, as Jo diminishes "To bone? To air? To dust?" (p. 61), but these needs threaten to render him impotent in responding to Jo's. He resents, though, any intrusion from others who might try to fulfill some of his role for him. Perhaps understandably, yet surely self-indulgently, he needs to be the only sufferer. If Elisabeth Kübler-Ross, in *On Death and Dying,* is correct in positing that the survivor must undergo the same stages as the victim in eventually arriving at an acceptance of death, then Sam cannot make that leap to detachment, which involves a growth from thinking only of one's self to selflessness.[8] Although the Lady from Dubuque assures him, "you don't know what it *is,*" Sam sobs, "I'm dying" (p. 157). For in Albee's dramas, the survivors exist under a peculiar burden not felt by the victims: not only must they live seeing the process of dying, but they must continue on after the death and the finality which means aloneness. They must, in short, suffer *after* the suffering has ceased for the dead. As the widowed Long-Winded Lady in *Box and Quotations* notes: "But what about *me!* ... I ... *am* left ... his dying is all over; all gone, but his *death* stays ... *he* had only his dying. I have both."[9]

Yet, the crux of Sam's suffering is not that he will go on alone, though that is surely a part of it, or even that he evidently has no religious belief to sustain him — though in any case religion is most often, in Albee, simply one of the many illusions that man falls back on.[10] Rather, it is Sam's inability to plumb the mystery of "things [he] would not be expected to understand" (p. 102), to know what the moment of death will be like. He desires the certainty that, at the point of her death, Jo have "No time to be afraid" (p. 160—and by extension that he, too, will not have time for fear either. And although Elizabeth grants him that assurance, he can still not be absolutely certain of that fact. What is proffered in place of that certainty, or of any hope grounded in a religious system, is the fact of a multi-layered reality. Since, in Pirandello-fashion, Sam can know neither his own identity (either in games or in life) nor that of death, all he can hope to know and all he needs to know is that existence moves not just on a literal but, ritualistically, on a symbolic, metaphoric, and archetypal plane as well.

Within *The Lady from Dubuque*, Albee alludes explicitly to Pirandello's *It Is So! (If You Think So!)*. When Elizabeth remarks to Sam, "You have a woman upstairs. You *say* she is your wife; I say she is my daughter" (p. 95), we recall the tension between Signor Ponza and his mother-in-law Signora Frola over the identity of Signora Ponza. Ponza claims that his wife is not Signora Frola's daughter, but instead his second wife who simply pretends, for the sake of the older woman, to be her deceased daughter. Signora Frola, on the other hand, insists that Ponza has only been deluded into thinking that her daughter is his second wife in order to assuage the guilt he feels over having treated her so badly that she needed to be sent to a sanatarium. The other characters in Pirandello's play demand to know the absolute truth about Signora Ponza's identity, not really for the sake of the truth but because they are meddling busybodies intent on settling on a single, comfortable interpretation of observable phenomena, without regard for the family's suffering and vulnerability. They demand that reality not be relative, that identity be fixed and not fluid, that existence be knowable. For Pirandello, however—and herein resides the existential dilemma in his drama—truth is multiple and subjective, as he insists when he has Signora Ponza say at the close of the play that she is both Signora Frola's daughter *and* Ponza's second wife. And it is such hallmarks of Pirandellianism as the multiplicity of personality and the relativity of truth that Albee carries over into his own drama. *Dubuque's* Oscar, in the fragmentation and adaptability of his role and personality, is analogous, finally, to Signora Ponza. Even before the dying Jo mistakes him for Sam come to her aid in her last moments, Oscar has been quite willing to shift his identity to meet the demands and objections of the other characters: when Edgar, for example, refuses to believe that Oscar learned judo while serving in the Foreign Legion, Oscar replies, "Then I *wasn't* in the Foreign Legion, I don't care" (p. 122).

That so much of the surface action in *The Lady from Dubuque* revolves around game-playing puts us in mind of the mask/wearer dichotomy and the life/theatre and stage/world metaphors that abound in Pirandello's plays. For instance, Albee structures one of his games as a play-within-the-play in which Sam and Carol gull the other characters who are then cast as an outraged audience to their ruse. Carol returns from the powder room, feigning the violated maiden in exaggerated fashion and claiming that Sam has attempted to seduce her. By playing this role, she manages to elicit a response of threatened manhood from her fiancé Fred, who can see nothing but the surface appearance which he immediately accepts as the truth. Fred's outraged reaction is only a humorous inversion and reduction of the kind of hysteria which everyone experiences when his or her own certainty is shaken. In his already tense condition, Sam, when faced with the unexpected appearance of Elizabeth and Oscar, is especially susceptible to anxiety over the unknown. Verbally, Albee underscores the convergence of his concerns with those of Pirandello by having Carol "dogmatic[ally], if uncertain[ly]" proclaim, "Things are either true or they're not" (p. 134) as if reality were amenable to a kind of either/or simplification instead of the both/and complexity which characterizes the human predicament. When Elizabeth insists that "Everything is true" (p. 160), she demands the same sort of acquiescence to subjective reality that Signora Ponza does. Yet if, for Pirandello, such assent to the multiplicity of truth renders each person's reality as "real" as that of the next—leaving every person with at least the assurance of his or her own subjective certainty — for Albee the suspicion always remains that if, indeed, "Everything is true," then "nothing is true" (p. 160). All solipsistically perceived realities become just another of the many illusions we depend upon to see us through life. If, for Pirandello's characters, there still exists the possibility for attaining individual certainty among an infinite number of relativities, for Albee's, on the other hand, even that much certainty seems in doubt and is, perhaps, just a desperate grasping after straws.

Thus, like several earlier Albee characters—(Harry and Edna from *Delicate Balance* and Leslie and Sarah from *Seascape* (1975) among them)—our Lady from Dubuque and her companion demand to be perceived on something other than just the literal level, as is clearly apparent from the text. First, instead of coming in through the doors which are used by the other characters, Elizabeth and Oscar "enter the set from one side, *from without the set*" (emphasis added). Moreover, Elizabeth's first line "we *are* in time" (p. 73), is ambiguous in the way that many lines in the later Albee are: It may mean that they have arrived before Jo dies, but it might just as well, especially given Albee's own emphasis on the word "*are*," indicate that they have entered the dimension of time from somewhere out of time. Sam's persistent question when he comes upon them the next morning, "Who are you?"—uttered ten times in four pages—linguistically echoes the line that the other characters addressed to Sam at the beginning of the first act when they were playing the game of Twenty Questions with each guest assuming an identity which the others tried to ascertain. As though he were still playing the guessing game from the night before, Sam now asks Elizabeth if she claims to be Jo's mother. Clearly, Elizabeth does not appear to be she; Jo's mother, we are told, is "tiny, thin as a rail, blue eyes —darting furtive blue eyes... pale hair, tinted pink, balding a little" (p. 20), whereas the character description tells us Elizabeth is "a stylish, elegant, handsome woman" (p. vii). Furthermore, Elizabeth hails from Dubuque rather than New Jersey. A mythical creation of *New Yorker* editor Harold Ross, the Lady from Dubuque became an archetype of the kind of reader the magazine was supposedly not appealing to and refused to play down to. She is, thus, an imaginary creature who has entered into the collective imagination and who is talked about as if she really existed. Jo, it is true, does feel that her real mother has deserted her; yet if no reason exists for believing that Elizabeth is Jo's mother, there is, as one of the guests comments, just as little reason for believing that she is not. Like the endless riddle of the model and the mansion in *Tiny Alice*, the Pirandellian drama of Elizabeth's "true" identity can never be resolved and is never intended to be. Analogically, however, Elizabeth is the archetypal mother to whose care Jo returns at death. The ambiguously inflected "Dear, great God, woman" (p. 78) which Sam addresses to Elizabeth might be heard not as a profane expletive but rather as a reverent epithet. In the dream vision which Elizabeth recounts, she talks of seagulls, surf, and the sunset — all images for freedom and death.

Oscar, who might be seen as a kind of "angel of death" in the tradition of that character from Albee's early playlet *The Sandbox*

(1959), assumes Sam's role as helpmate to Jo as she crosses the threshold from dying to death. Dressed like Sam in his distinctive sleeping gown, "arms wide, beatific," Oscar asks: "Am I not...am I, indeed, not Sam?" (p. 153). In the game at the opening of the play, Sam had pretended that he was Romulus and Remus; at the close of the play, Oscar is, in a sense, Sam's twin: morally he performs the action which Sam is incapable of undertaking. He possesses a strength which Sam lacks, carrying Jo up the stairs for the last time and easing her into death. If Elizabeth is the Lady from Dubuque and archetypal mother, Oscar is the comforting angel Sam fails to be. Since Sam cannot really be a husband to Jo in her need, that role is fulfilled by Oscar, who is his double. And just as, ironically, this Lady from Dubuque is more cognizant and knowing than the other characters, so, too, Oscar—though black—is not a demonic twin or double. If he is the Romulus who "kills" or replaces the Remus/Sam, it is only because Jo cannot wait for Sam's help.

At the very end, Sam is still asking Elizabeth, "Who are you? Really?" (p. 161). Of course, not knowing himself, he cannot possibly hope to know the other. The bedrock question remains the Sphinx's "Who am I" since "all of the [other] values [are] relative save" that (p. 152), But then, to reach any certitude about who one is and who another is in Albee, as in Pirandello, is an impossible dream. What Sam might more profitably have done was to probe the fuller dimensions of existence by confronting the Lady from Dubuque with the question: "Who are you, metaphorically?" That, perhaps, would have been a first step in approaching the ineffable mystery at the very heart of existence —something that Carol, who began as the most bewildered of all the guests, seems able to do. She intuitively senses who and what the Lady from Dubuque and Oscar are, grasps what is happening, and honestly tries to help Sam help Jo. To see anagogically, to perceive existence as multi-leveled, is Albee's only answer to the problem of knowing that he poses in his plays. To remain always on the level of the literal reality (unknowable as even that level is) is, indeed, "too little." To know metaphorically, symbolically, archetypally is, to paraphrase Hemingway, what humankind in Albee has instead of God. Toast may be just toast, but it might also be heaven.

Notes

[1]The general tenor of the reviews which greeted the New York production of the play is best seen in the title of John Simon's review, "From Hunger, Not Dubuque," *New York* 13 (11 February 1980):74–75. Other reviews include Walter Kerr, "Stage: Albee's 'Lady from Dubuque,'" *New York Times* (1 February 1980), C-5; Clive Barnes, *The New York Post* (1 February 1980), p. 33; Robert Brustein, "Self-Parody and Self-Murder," *The New Republic* 182 (8 March 1980):26–27; and Jack Kroll, "Going to Hell with Albee," *Newsweek* 95 (11 February 1980):pp. 102–3.

[2]Otis L. Guernsey, Jr., *The Best Plays of 1979–80* (New York: Dodd, Mead, 1980), pp. 4, 15.

[3]Edward Albee, *Tiny Alice* (New York: Atheneum, 1980), p. 107. Further page references appear in the text.

[4]Edward Albee, *Counting the Ways and Listening: Two Plays* (New York: Atheneum, 1977), pp. 5, 51. Subsequent page references to both plays appear in the text.

[5]The topos of "game playing" has, of course, long been recognized as an important element in Albee's works. Studies range from Elmer Hankiss, "Who's Afraid of Edward Albee?" *New Hungarian Quarterly* 5 (Autumn 1964):168–74 (Game as a device for revealing the emptiness of life) and Louis Paul, "A Game Analysis of Albee's *Who's Afraid of Virginia Woolf?*: The Core of Grief," *Literature and Psychology* 17 (1967):47–51 (games as a psychological device to avoid problems such as the emptiness of life), to the recent study by Cynthia B. Thomiszer, "Child's Play: Games in *The Zoo Story*," *College Literature* (1982):54–63.

[6]Pirandellian aspects in Albee's work have already been noted by Dan Sullivan in "Ill-fated *Breakfast at Tiffany's*," *New York Times*, 15 December 1966, p. 6. Sullivan calls the work "an exercise in Pirandello style about fiction and reality."

[7]Edward Albee, *The Lady from Dubuque* (New York: Atheneum, 1980), p. ix. Further page references appear in the text.

[8]See Elisabeth Kübler-Ross, M.D., *On Death and Dying* (New York: Macmillan, 1969).

[9]Edward Albee, *Box* and *Quotations from Chairman Mao Tse-tung* (New York: Pocket Books, 1970), pp. 88–9.

[10]For discussions of Albee's attitude toward religious belief, see C. W. E. Bigsby, *Confrontation and Commitment: A Study of Contemporary American Drama, 1959–1966* (Kansas City: University of Missouri Press, 1967), pp. 85–92, as well as Samuel Terrien, "Demons Also Believe: Parodying the Eucharist," *Christian Century*, 9 December 1970, pp. 1481–83.

Edward Albee's *Counting the Ways*
The Ways of Losing Heart

PHILIP C. KOLIN

O FFERING AN ASSESSMENT/APOLOGIA for the plays of Albee's "middle period," Clive Barnes, in his review of *Counting the Ways*, noted, "As Mr. Albee progresses, he gets more and more interested in mechanics, the special workings of the theatre. The play rejects the fiction of the essential theatrical transaction that is meant to take place in a vacuum."[1] Indeed, the general critical appraisal of Albee's *Counting the Ways* is that the random collection of skits that comprise the play seems to lack a center, that *Counting the Ways* is a play turned inside out where what should be the center is on the surface. To be sure, there is quite clearly no central action, as in *All Over*, or metaphor, as in *Tiny Alice*, from which all else could be said to emanate. Rather than having a central idea dictating the form of its own expression, the reverse appears to be the case in *Counting the Ways*. What has bothered critics the most is that the play seems centripetal rather than centrifugal in its nature, with the seemingly unconnected series of skits and blackouts having been lashed together in some unknown fashion in one of the less accessible corners of the playwright's creative vision. Thus, Douglas Watt, in the *New York Daily News*, was typical in his complaint that "Form seems more and more to dominate content so that love and its infinite variations, one of the playwright's major concerns, are here imprisoned in a kind of cloudy aspic."[2] However, Watt's complaint of a lack of clarity is based on what he believes should be readily perceptible to the eyes of critic and playgoer alike, for his judgment is built on the presupposition of the primacy of content and the secondary, auxiliary, function of form. This curious contention in the relative values of "mechanics," or "form," and content is best seen in the contradictory reviews which greeted the 1977 Albee-directed American debut of *Counting the Ways*. While the majority of reviews were savagely negative in regard to the play's content, most reviewers, even those vigorously negative about the play, found purpose and a guiding hand in Albee's direction,[3] which was termed by one critic, "lucid and deliberate."[4]

However, the paradox between a "meaningless" play and its purposeful production is resolved when one realizes that the complexity and deliberateness of its form were intended to be contrasted to its seeming lack of content, for the tension between form and content is a reflection of the play's subject matter which is the state of modern marriage.[5] In Albee's eyes, such marriages are essentially hollow, consisting of little substance and subsisting on a great many quirky forms and games. Hence, in his portrayal of families, Albee consistently insists on calling his characters by generic or functional names, such as "Mommy" and "Daddy," rather than personal ones. In the same fashion, the two characters who populate *Counting the Ways*, "He" and "She," act out only the roles ascribed to them by virtue of their genders. They, like the play itself, are deliberately formless beings without centers. They are collections of manners and mannerisms imposed from without who act without benefit of personalities. In the final analysis, *Counting the Ways* is concerned with just that lack or loss of meaning—in marriage, in life, in art—and with the resultant reliance on empty forms which such losses inevitably entail. There is no doubt that the play's anonymous couple is obsessed with finding out what words, actions, feelings, and thoughts mean. Throughout the play, they define, decode, and decipher in a futile attempt to establish meanings; yet inevitably they must take their only solace from the form rather than from the elusive object of their quest.

The ways in which Albee counts the loss of meaning in the couple's lives is best seen in the play's subtitle, "A Vaudeville," which draws attention to the particular form in which the dialogue is cast. The choice of this once popular form of entertainment suggests the atmosphere and structural qualities which Albee needed in order to reproduce the meaninglessness in his couple's lives. Vaudeville represents the nadir to which He and She have descended. A vaudevillian love is a slapstick love—one battered and bruised with insults, gags, and surrounded by banter. Moreover, vaudeville thrives on parody and frequently offers a parody of itself. Indeed, antiquated burlesque nicely characterizes the aging pair's search for meaning. In fact, *Counting the Ways* parodies romantic comedy, vaudeville-style. The quest of a romantic comedy is to find out if boy loves girl and *vica versa*. This is the very type of love which is the subject of the 1957 romantic sex comedy, "Love in the Afternoon," the title of which is the same as that of the song which becomes the momentary focal point of the couple's sexual banter as He and She explore the phrase's euphemistic possibilities. In the end, no satisfactory explanation of the title's meaning is achieved, and when He demands to know what "Love in the Afternoon" really means, She can only respond with the evasive, "Call 'em up; find out."[6] The escapades of the movie which starred Gary Cooper, Audrey Hepburn, and Maurice Chevalier comically contrast with the events in the lives of He and She. "Love in the Afternoon" portrays the philandering mishaps of a man who is warned by the daughter of a private detective about the vengeful plans of a jealous husband. Perhaps that kind of jealous vengeance is hinted at in the closing lines of the play which refer to a madman's breaking into He's and She's house with a machete. The sexual intrigue which the movie allusion suggests reminds the audience that no such entanglements and passions confront this sexually sedentary couple. In his use of vaudevillian form, Albee intentionally burlesques the form and substance of such romantic comedies. His lovers are neither young nor idealistic. The games they play are based on traditional love tests which for them are either absurd or have no meaning. Such games are foolishly enacted and even more outlandishly interpreted. In the end, neither boy nor girl possesses each other, and there are no escapades for this lifeless couple who stand stiffly and woodenly deliver their comic patter in the exaggerated form of vaudeville.

There are, of course, several other ways in which the overtly vaudevillian form of the play deliberately serves both to create and shape the presentation of the sterile vacuity which characterizes the lives of He and She. The traditional bareness of the vaudevillian stage and the starkness of vaudevillian stage business, provide an appropriate backdrop and commentary on He's and She's maneuvers to escape intimacy. In the Hartford production, directed by Albee, the deliberate use of what Barnes termed "mechanics" as a way of creating "meaning" was particularly evident. David Jenkins' sparse set consisted of two chairs, a table, and a "series of greyish textured trapezoidal screens that gave *Counting the Ways* the look of a set for television."[7] Similarly, Clive Barnes remarked that "the scene is as bare as a quiz show."[8] Against such a set He and She play their quizzical games. The set captures the doubt, the impersonality, the absurdity of indifference, and the meaninglessness that have crept into their marriage. It is the external representation of their inward state. Also effective in creating an environment devoid of meaning and warmth are the blackouts which, throughout the play, separate its twenty-one scenes from each other. Vaudeville-inspired, these blackouts reveal the separateness, the apartness-on-stage, that is within He and She. Ironically, the very aspects which most disturbed the critics may be meaningful as commentary on the status of the two characters. We are supposed to be bothered by these aspects of the play just as we are supposed to be bothered by aspects of He's and She's lives.

The limited action on that stage also shows He and She desiring to escape the responsibilities of intimacy. Appropriately, the play opens with no one on stage — a foreboding sign descends, announcing the production, so that the play begins with emptiness and ends with uncertainty. Once the characters do appear, their sometimes unconscious quest for separation begins. Seated across from each other at a table, He and She might possibly present a cozy, domestic scene. But they appear more like adversaries in an affair of the heart than models of wedded love. That adversarial role is made even more dramatic at the beginning of Scene 2, where "They both have moved to standing positions, each to one side of the stage, near their exitway" (p. 7). At safe distances from each other, He and She resemble overweight pugilists ready for a hefty if comic sparring match. Many of the remaining scenes also stress the couple's separation and self-encapsulation. Scenes open with one or the other character talking, only to be joined by the partner who either refuses to listen or retreats quickly offstage. Calling attention to She's escape from him, He has to speak "Louder, so She will hear, offstage" (p. 19). The two most glaring instances of such separation resulting from fear of intimacy occur in Scenes 12 and 13. After refusing at first to give her a rose, a traditional symbol of love intentionally downgraded to a vaudevillian prop, He stands holding a rose: "Eyes still closed. He makes a grimace, extends, shakes his flower-held arm even further" (p. 21). He holds a sign of love at arm's length for She to grasp. Not desirous of even a touch of her hand, He wants to externalize and hence remove affection. In Scene 13, He opens by standing "alone on stage, holding the flowers." From a safe retreat backstage, She "pokes her head in," admonishing him that "They're going to wilt!" (p. 27). The separation they sense in their lives is also symbolized through lighting. He is stationed center stage while She hides in the "yawning blackness of the backstage area."[9] Later, when they are on stage together, She leaves, and He asks, "Where are you going?". She shows her lack of emotional involvement by answering with a laconic, "Off" (p. 36).

The physical space between the scenes of the play and between the characters' lives is, of course, symbolic of the emotional emptiness of their married life. Space erupts in that life as an inevitable consequence of their escape from intimacy and their journey toward meaninglessness. His reaction to her announcement about separate beds is delayed rather than immediate. Such hesitation weakens the force of her statement and robs the problem of its immediacy and, hence, its status as a "crisis." He inquires, "When did it happen? When did our lovely bed split and become two? When did a table appear where there has been no space, in the center of our lovely bed?" (p. 33). Audiences may well recall the separating table of Scene 1. Playing the role of a meliorist, She tries to calm him by noting that "Maybe we'll be lucky and it won't go any further" and progress to separate rooms. But the change to separate rooms seems imminent. Unequivocally, the separate beds will prohibit any possibility for intimacy and thereby afford a convenient excuse for separate rooms. But the change in sleeping accommodations forebodes a more serious problem. He observes of the two beds: "They're not wide, those beds; they're single; they're for a solitary, or for a corpse" (p. 34). Escaping intimacy, they have moved closer toward isolation and death.

In representing the dissolution of the marriage, Albee consistently evokes the number two as a symbol of disunity, separation, and ultimately death in *Counting the Ways*. In both allusion and structure, the play is clearly designed to heighten the audience's awareness that isolation—that is, separation or duality—is the ultimate cause of the couple's feelings of emptiness and despair. Thus, within the play, everything destructive seems to come in twos. That this is a two-character play hardly seems incidental. The one marriage disintegrates into two separate and frayed human beings whose flight from each other leads to grave isolation. She and He each have an "exitway." She has her coffee; He has his tea. In order to cancel any complementary expression of love, She does not want each of them to have a rose (p. 20). The possibility of reunion through the two desserts—creme brulée and raspberry fool—is doomed; they are out of both. Moreover, the sexual delights of creme brulée lead to the ridicule of raspberry fool anyway. The number two is a *memento mori* for their own mortality and their failed dreams. As She says, "There are two things: cease and corruption" (p. 8). Appropriately, She tells two stories, each focusing on losses. In her first story, She recounts what happened at a prom where She was admired by two boys from whom She received two gardenias. But the two suitors led to no permanent relationship: "No, I didn't marry him [her date]—the shy boy either" (p. 25). All that she reaps from the encounter with the two boys is a painful memory of the shy boy when She makes love. In her second story, She agonizes over the protocol of seating two men, each dying of cancer. Friends of her family, these men offer more than a problem with protocol. Albee uses them to suggest that She is blind to the mortality they represent in her life. Protocol, form, is merely a useful sanctuary in which She can escape the monstrous reality which her guests represent. The blunt husband also resorts to the use of duality in order to characterize loss and destruction. In repeating what He has heard about man's exhaustible supply of life-producing semen, He notes: "Ya only got a coupla thousand in ya; don't waste it in ya hand!" (p. 43).

The emphasis on twos inevitably leads Albee to the use of repetition, parallelism, and counterpoint. In fact, the pervading sense of duality, a type of diptych of the absurd, is built into the action of the play and accounts for much of its structure,[10] and it is these structural devices which become the "missing" plot or substance—that is, meaning —of the play. Such a binary structure was doubtless suggested by Albee's own interest in music. He has said that "The only model I have is music" and has even supplied an actual source for Counting the Ways: "piano pieces by Satie."[11] The repetitions in Counting the Ways are therefore analogous to the repetitions of "themes" in classical music. They bear a structural similarity to leitmotifs, contrapuntal orchestrations, or sonata-like movements. But the similarity extends to form, not to function or meaning. Whereas a contrapuntal musical score emphasizes unity through diversity, Albee's parallels underscore the couple's estrangement, not unity, which even extends at times to parody. The parallels enact the same message of alienation as do the references to twos. Albee's parallels proclaim the fatuousness of a life that may be shared but not communicated. They reveal that people do not listen to each other. Failed communication, especially between people who should have a strong and sustaining emotional relationship, has shaped much of Albee's work. In the interview printed earlier in this volume, Albee traces his interest in the "rapid breakdown in communication" back to the American Dream. He observes: "People just don't listen. That's why Mommy was able to say to Mrs. Barker, 'Won't you take off your dress,' rather than 'Won't you take off your coat.' ... one doesn't listen and doesn't pay attention."[12] Albee continues by saying that "to a large extent" *Listening* was about the same problem. A recognition of the parallels in *Counting the Ways* shows that He and She are in a revolving door where there is movement and sound but no progress or togetherness.

Another humorous structural parallel that Albee exploits for its contrapuntal effect concerns the stage business with the roses. Both She and He walk on stage, separately, each carrying a rose. He is first in Scenes 10 and 11; She follows in Scene 12. The parallel entrances underscore the absurdity of the couple's relationship. Neither He nor She is an appropriate flower-bearer, especially of a flower emblematic of love and romance. The fact that She follows him with a rose in her hand may indicate that they are both in search of the same thing. But, as was seen, She recoils from their mutual possession of a rose (or a badge of love); She wants to deprive one of them of all roses and thus thwart any shared activity. In another action involving the roses, She strives to undo whatever message they give her husband. In Scene 7, He plucks the petals from a rose in playing the game of "She loves me; she loves me not" (p. 14). Two scenes later, She discovers the defoliated rose and attempts to restore its petals, and as She puts them back, with very little success, She repeats the words backwards. It is as if She does not want her husband to find out the true answer such a test may give, or perhaps she wants to undo whatever talismanic spell the roses may have cast over him, especially *if* He received an answer that would force her to agree. The absurdity of repeating, in reverse, her husband's actions is part of her quest to circumvent emotional confrontations.

Albee continues to orchestrate such structural parallels between the two of them to show how insulated each has become. Both characters recount stories from their youth, but without any indication that they understand or even listen to each other. Both their vignettes focus on earlier love affairs and both stress flowers—his are dandelions and daisies; hers are gardenias. Now He cannot recall why they blew dandelions into the air and wonders "Was it for love?" (p. 19). A great deal of distance lies between those affairs of the heart and his present life. She, too, remembers an event which might have been for love, although her story of the two boys seems like a less sentimental version of his experiences. He, at least, is willing to concede that his actions may have been for love. She allows no such feeling to color her rendition of how a gardenia smells "once it gets the body heat" (p. 23). She recalls with displeasure: "nowadays their scent makes me faintly ill" (p. 22). His inability to remember the uses to which they put the dandelions contrasts with her vivid and pungent recollection of the flower's odor.

The revelations, if they can be called that, lead not to mutual understanding about each other's psychic past but rather to studies in separation. That He and She both find time to quote from authorities on Love is yet another example of such parallels whose initial promise of reconcilliation, upon closer scrutiny, is seen as an underscoring of the finality of the couple's estrangement. Parallel lines, far from being symbols of harmony or proximity are, rather, emblems of those things which are irrevocably separate. She remembers what her grandmother (always a venerable figure in Albee) has said about love: *"love* doesn't die; we pass *through* it" (p. 11). An obvious counterpoint to this sentiment is found in his quoting the old experts about love: "ya only got a coupla thousand in ya; don't waste it in ya hand" (p. 43). Both observations focus on the transitory nature of love. But ironically, his comment derogates hers by rendering it in the most graphic and literal terms. Neither character, however, profits from whatever small wisdom can be gleaned from these amorous aphorisms since He and She fail to apply these observations to self or to spouse.

Just as the parallels point to the contradictions in the characters' lives, so too does their language. One of the symptoms of the dissolution of a marriage is seen in the characters' inability to raise or to respond to questions. The ability to raise such questions is at the core of a successful marriage, according to Albee. In a recent interview, he linked the interrogative mode with family health: "There are several ways for families to hang together. One is to ask no questions. Another is to ask all questions. When you ask no questions, you hang together until you just disintegrate and aren't aware the disintegration is taking place and if you ask all questions you may possibly recreate a family structure but with firmer bonding."[13]

Clearly, in Albee's view, a healthy marriage depends upon being able to communicate with one's partner in order to be aware of one's own self. Questions create a discourse between asker and answerer. They lead to unity rather than separateness. One need only note that He and She have trouble with questions — large or small; questions are threatening. He is incapable of asking her if She loves him—"Why didn't you just ask me?" (p. 15) She demands after He has circumvented her with his petal-picking test for "She loves me; she loves me not." The playwright uses this question of love as yet another structuring device the purpose of which is to demonstrate the lack of meaning which is the play's principal theme. *Counting the Ways* begins and closes with the same question—"Do you love Me?" It is She who asks it in Scene 1 and He who responds perfunctorily with a "Hm? Pardon?"

(p. 5), a little dismayed at being asked any question, let alone this one. The situation of doubt is seemingly reversed at the end of the play when He admits "I do love you. Let well enough alone. If it's well enough...let it alone" (p. 51). She then echoes his response of Scene 1: "Hmmm." And when He asks if She does love him, her answer is uncertain. Nothing changes between these two questions; the repetition marks stasis. The feared question is again asked when She quickly inserts it at the end of her list:

> Walnuts!
> Parsley!
> Bone marrow!
> Celery root!
> CREME BRULÉE.
> > *(Pause; enthusiasic)*
> Do you love me?! (p. 7).

She intentionally deflates the importance of the query by placing it in such an unemotional, mundane context. Hoping that the question will either be overlooked or that it will not lead to a lengthy, revealing discussion, She tries to control his response, thus disclosing her own uncertainty and lack of trust. She equivocates in both wanting to know and conceal the answer. As if to parody her list, He repeats it verbatim when He searches for words—"something in the middle"—with which to change the line from Auden (p. 26). The twist, though, is that He supplies an answer of sorts—"Thousands have lived without love, but none without Creme Brulée." Since they have run out of that delicacy (an Albeean objective correlative for love?), surely the repetition of the list points only to the futility of any love. Whether it is about love or, as we shall see, poetry, their shared list is, like protocol, an empty form which serves to protect them from each other and from unpleasant realities.

Amid their fragmented and momentary conversations, the characters seek isolation, not a union, of selves. That is why questions, with the discourse they create, are such threats to He and She. In place of discourse or dialogue, they substitute two monologues, each set apart from the other. She, in particular, becomes her own self-parody through her closed linguistic system. In She, Albee recreates the woman who so often in his plays lives by the rules of a sterile formality. She strives for perfection, order, and specificity in her language. For her, language must be rigidly precise, tabulated, and codified. She banishes the spontaneity of natural creation which accounts for language's vitality and variety in order to impose an artificial and externally derived order on a world falling apart. Her list of walnuts, parsley, bone marrow, and celery curiously ends with creme brulée. The first four ingredients represent things natural, productive (in fact aphrodisiacal;) to which is joined the sophisticated dessert which becomes a symbol of lost love. Her chant—litany, if you will—of these ingredients shows her attempt to harness life forces and reduce them to artificiality, conventionalism. The list could well be considered the antithesis of a fertility chant. Intentionally, it is anticlimatic, pointing to the emotional sterility of her marriage.

With an exactitude which belies neurotic compulsion, She qualifies, modifies, and categorizes what She says. Recalling her prom night, She pinpoints for the audience exactly where her date placed the gardenia corsage—"above my left breast, and a little low, sort of...on it rather than above it." (p. 22). Identifying the shy boy, She speaks with documentary coldness: "I sensed him ... or who he proved to be" (p. 23). She speaks as if She fears being interrupted by anyone with a question or a qualification. She talks about two cancer-stricken friends of the family with a minimum of emotion: "Two of the guests are dying —well we all are, but these two are closer to it" (p. 40). Maintaining her guard, She twice qualifies a remark concerning what everyone knows about proper protocol: "You would think—*one* would think, *might* think ..." (p. 40). She is very self-conscious about linguistic *faux pas*, a sign of her concern with appearances. Describing the departure of the shy boy, She observes: "And scram he did, if one can do it slowly" (p. 25). She wonders if it is more proper to say "close-knit family...or closely knit" (p. 40). When She thinks a word or a phrase is particularly apt, She announces it smugly: "a bit of ... pudge. That's a nice way to put it," referring to young girl's complexion (p. 22). And when She recalls that the shy boy stood, "looking down at me with a sort of... puzzled hurt" (p. 23), She acknowledges her talent at making language precise and clever, at least for her.

Yet despite her preoccupation with choosing the right word, She repeatedly is rebuffed by linguistic uncertainty. She grapples with the meaning of phrases years after they have been uttered. She still wonders about the shy boy's words to her—"See you" as She asks, "Does 'See you' mean something more? Does 'See you' mean 'I suspect you're inviting me, subtly, of course, and naturally I accept'? Does 'See you' mean *that*? It *must!*" (p. 24). When the intent behind words may waver,

She forcefully restricts them to the meaning She thinks they should have. She wryly crushes metaphor in her crucible of decorum when explaining to He what "Love in the afternoon"means: "It means sex in the afternoon." Jesting with her husband, She continues to interpret the meaning of the phrase: "Sure: love means sex; eyes are thighs; lips mean hips. I kiss your lips means ... " (p. 9). When He replies that "Nobody ever said that," She retorts, "Still...it's what it means." Balking at "the limpid pools of your thighs," He is admonished: "Don't be literal" (p. 10). Yet ironically, it is She who is doggedly literal-minded, and if He is still in doubt, it is He who should "Call 'em up; find out."

In other criticisms of her husband's speech, She reveals the same dedication to a reasoned coldness. In the midst of their discussion of single beds, She tells him to respond "with calm and reason" (p. 29). When He summons up enough courage to admit "I wake up this morning ... in our kingsize bed" (p. 30) and start a discussion, She disarms him with the following comment: "You've moved into the historical present, I hope you realize." She is more concerned with the tense (the form) than the message (the substance). She adds: "It's an odd tense, isn't it—sort of common, if you know what I mean. It's useful, I know, but...*still.*" However "useful" She says the tense is, it presents a danger for her because it telescopes the past (in which they did love) into the present (where they do not). She cannot accept blending the two, for that will lead to giving reasons, explanations requiring an exposure of self. She wants to separate the past and the present, to keep the emotions of the past from creeping into the present and, most of all, into the future. The husband's tense will not allow her to date and dispose of an emotional attachment quickly. Moving from the role of grammarian to that of philosopher, She will require of him an epistemological justification: "How do you know you love me?" (p. 50). When He invents the story of the man with a machete, She overlooks his desire for rapprochement, brands him as "silly," and urges him to "Be reasonable." She has not learned that love and reason must obey different rules.

However, her rational veneer is quite transparent. Despite her linguistic exactitude, when it comes to employing language for the matters of the heart, She often is incapable of being decisive, accurate, or even logical. When She asks at the beginning of the play if He loves her, She almost surreptitiously slips the question in at the end of her list. When He asks if She wants an answer at once, She vacillates and is incapable of the precision characterizing her other statements: "Well... *yes.* Or...no, no, not really. *Yes*" (p. 6). The same instability, reflecting a fear of communication and intimacy, surfaces when He wants to discuss why there is a space between the beds. At first She affirms, "I don't want to discuss it!" and adds, "I do not wish to discuss it!" and still a little later agrees "Well; let us sit down and discuss it" (pp. 28–29). One of the emotional symbols of their love, the children, also causes her to waver. How many children do they have—three or four? She is not sure (pp. 41–42). Finally, She concludes the play with indecision. She does not know if She loves him but says, "I think I do" (p. 51. Her last words, especially the verb *think*, mock her reliance on rational discovery and clear-cut protocol. Her "think" is a weak and parodical version of a language centered on sterile thought and not on warm feeling.

To a far lesser extent, He parodies himself, too. Possibly because He comes from a long line of passive males in Albee's plays, He is less vocal and, hence, less vulnerable. But like She, He cannot adhere to a consistent means of expression. Being discovered by the audience after He picks the rose petals, He runs and hides. Later, He poses as an expert public speaker, ready to offer a learned discourse on "premature grief" as he "Clears his throat [and] speaks to the audience" (p. 37). The almost manic switch from nursing his inhibitions and escaping notice to declaiming publicly on how to grieve ahead of time shows his own emotional uncertainty about love and himself. Nor is he apprehensive or taciturn when He can parody (and thus diminish) poetry. In front of the audience, He congratulates himself on changing the Auden line. With her, He acts in the same inconsistent way. He can quarrel with her about how long they have been married — He says seven; She says six years (p. 3), a difference of opinion demanding comparison with her uncertainty about the number of children they have. But at times He is frozen into silence. Deciding to leave when She speaks about protocol, He is "All tight-lipped and clenched and ready to start muttering," or at least so She says (p. 39).

Not only are He and She inconsistent and insincere in using their own language, but they treat the language of others ambiguously through a peculiar use of allusion, particularly literary allusion. The allusions in *Counting the Ways* have been judged solely as a reflection of Albee's indiscriminate reading.[14] But it is necessary to examine Albee's dialogue dramatically rather than biographically, for the criticism leveled at the author is more applicable to his characters. Mark Boyer has found that the allusion-filled speeches of He and She are characteristic of the way Albeeites talk; their speech is "an elevated and epigrammatic version of small talk."[15] Such a view is consistent with Albee's own perceptions of his characters' language. In a 1979 interview, he acknowledged: "All my people are terribly articulate, they could communicate if they chose to. But they don't choose to."[15] This admission comes close to the truth of why and how allusions function in the play. They show how little impact literature has had on the lives of these upper middle class characters. Albee's characters fail to understand or respond to literature. Thomas Adler has said that references to art show how far characters in Albee have descended.[17] But even that view assumes that they can see the disparity between their lives and the enobling truth that art and literature have to offer, and no such vision exists in *Counting the Ways*. He and She just cite lines or parrot ideas without recognizing the emotional enrichment such allusions should provide. They are deaf and dumb aesthetically speaking, thus offering further proof of their failed communication. Since they have no personal understanding of the works they have read, the couple can neither speak nor listen with sincerity. For He and she, hunting for sources has become a parlor game. As She proves, *"Time?* That's *all* you have. Who *said* it?" and He responds, "Time? Too much and too little. I don't *know"* (p. 38). Such allusion hunting is mere diversion, for it never produces insight or even further commentary. Her answer to her own question is "Someone." On the surface, He and She appear to be highly educated, well-read individuals, just as George and Martha seem to be in *Who's Afraid of Virginia Woolf?*, but in reality He and She are like so many suburban couples who have a mandatory large and richly embossed tome on their coffee tables—for show and not scrutiny. Albee's point is that He and She employ intellectually or emotionally charged language without savoring its intent. Their allusions, lacking a central core of meaning and feeling, are like a microcosm of the play as a whole. Their allusions have form but not significance in the same way the play has rituals but not the guidance such rituals should provide. In other words, their apparent lack of meaning is the larger "meaning" of the play as a whole.

No clearer indication of this lack of aesthetic understanding occurs in the play than in He's switching the words of an Auden poem. He substitutes the domestic "shirts" for Auden's "water" in "Thousands have lived without love, but none without water" (p. 26). Unashamedly, He confesses that "I thought that was rather good, there, before, what I said." A little later He substitutes each of the ingredients from his wife's list for Auden's "water." When He exchanges "creme brulee" for "water," He does admit: "It lacks . . . well, it doesn't . . . there's not as much *resonance* that way . . . Creme Brulée for water, or *shirts* for water, for that matter, but if parody *isn't* a diminishment . . . well, then, was it worth it in the first place?" (p. 26). He and She deliberately parody serious ideas and words from poetry, thus showing little if any aesthetic appreciation for the material which they cite. Such are the people whom Albee consistently terms "Philistines" in his public addresses.

He claims a knowledge of Auden's poetry, but such claims are specious or unattuned to the work's meaning. He thinks that "probably" the line in question came from "In Praise of Limestone." But it does not. He says He cried three times in his life—at the death of Auden, the death of a cat, and at "something to do with civilization" (p. 27). The juxtaposition of a cat's death and Auden's seems like a ludicrous incongruity, to the poet's discredit. Moreover, something as specific as Auden's death appears dwarfed in light of the looming vagary of all civilization. The question to be asked is "Of what emotional value was Auden to him?" The answer is not very flattering. In fact, He even questions if He ever cried at the poet's death (p. 26). He imagines Auden's poetry, and the result is not appreciation but parody. Auden's poetry exists not for the insights or beauty which it offers but for the verbal tricks he can perform with it using his wife's list. He thinks of Auden's imagining a lover's death later in the play (p. 43). Auden's own grief as a lover is sincere and thereby contrasts with his cold, calculating grief: since He grieves "over her death, a little, every day," He will "have enough" when She does die (p. 42). As a hedge against the future, his grief is collected into a comfortable reservoir. The allusion to Auden thus points to the husband's shallowness and again causes an audience to question just how serious the loss of his wife would be to him.

At best, He and She merely parody literature. Albee has them inject lines of poetry or philosophical ideas in contexts which are patently humorous or whimsical. Without understanding or appreciating what they say, He and She appear even more ridiculous each time they are allusive. The most obvious illustration, from which the title of the play comes, occurs in Scene 21 where, in answer to her question asking him how He knows He loves her, He repeats the famous lines from Elizabeth Barrett Browning's poem: "How do I love thee?/Let me count the ways" (p. 49). Her response is "Be serious." He jocularly replies, "I thought she *was*." The sentiment expressed in these lines from Elizabeth Barrett Browning is totally absent in their lives, and at best the words of the poem lead to a stale joke. The synapses between poetry and love have been severed. Predicting that some day He will not be able to "'rise' to the occasion" because of waning sexual prowess, She provides comments about "the sudden void," adding a sarcastic "nevermore, as the bird said" (p. 8). These references to existentalism and Poe are signs of her aesthetic bankruptcy because She cannot differentiate their serious significance from the foolish humor of her joke about her husband's penis being like a piece of dough. In her use of literature, the apocalyptic becomes the bathetic. The two uses are the same for her. In the middle of their tepid argument about single beds, He asks, "We are each other's rod?" (p. 32). And She answers, "So to speak," a marvelously appropriate response given the fact that they try to taunt or abuse each other verbally. But their attempts are foolish. They use a word, "rod," which is traditionally charged with meaning, but they themselves are unaware of the passion and commitment it should have. In context, their being each other's rod suggests a faint allusion to Psalm 23 where God is both "rod" and "staff." According to the *Jerome Commentary*, "the vivid metaphors derived from shepherding cover all the contingencies of human life," e.g., the "rod" for "hostile beings," the "staff" for "sure guidance."[18] In saying that they are each other's rod, He timidly points to the pain which each of these hostile beings inflicts upon the other, but that pain seems like a needle prick compared to the suffering suggested by the allusion. Again, a mere shadow of a full allusion indicates just how ignorant they are about the feeling such allusions should instill and inspire. For a couple which has lost passion, passionate words lose meaning and all point of reference. Clearly, He's and She's allusions are empty; there is no core of feeling behind such allusive language.

It is, of course, fatal to mistake the attitudes of the characters for those of the playwright, yet that is exactly what has most frequently happened in the case of *Counting the Ways* as Albee has been pilloried for the allusional vacuity of his characters. George Rogoff, for example, charges: "The territory is familiar—the brittleness of Coward, the allusiveness of Pinter, and, even to my surprise, the distancing of Brecht. Or is it Pirandello this time—two characters in search of their elusive author? Albee used to be available, but now he seems to be locked in a monkish cell populated only by theatrical quotation and decorative words."[19] Yet Albee's use of such dramatic techniques is not necessarily a mark of bungling imitation or a sign of befuddled stagecraft. Albee purposely severs conventions from the meaning they have for an audience. In violating an audience's expectations, Albee shocks rather than soothes. The seeming staleness and the vacuity of the stagecraft are exactly the point of the play. They are the linchpins of the vaudevillian parody aimed at romantic comedy. Like the empty allusions placed within the mouths of the characters, the hollow, clumsily borrowed stagecraft of the larger context of "the play" is designed to reflect the emptiness of modern love by parodying the literature through which that love is portrayed. In affecting that parody, Albee uses stage conventions in much the same way he does allusions. Just as allusions reveal the characters' empty lives, so do conventions deprived of meaning point to the confusion in which He and She live. Albee transforms many of the conventions of the modern theatre — flashbacks, illusionary staging, psychosexual symbolism, distancing — by turning them upside down.

Finally, an instructive way in which to see how Albee has re-worked those conventions is to compare *Counting the Ways* with Tennessee Williams' *The Glass Menagerie*, the very type of romantic play of the heart at which Albee aims his vaudevillian parody, although in fairness one must note that Albee admires Williams as a playwright. Certainly it would be unfair to argue that Albee consciously strove to imitate or parody Williams, but in many ways Albee's play is a direct response to the kind of theatre of the heart projected by Williams. Clearly, *The Glass Menagerie* and *Counting the Ways* push aside the conventions of realism. Both plays can be called memory plays. For Williams, a depiction of memory "is seated predominantly in the heart,"[20] while for Albee memory is a non-emotional faculty. Both She and Amanda recount their girlhood memories of dances and dates, and to be sure, both women are the victims of frustration and dejection. But Amanda's account contrasts with the callous recollection given by She. Amanda luxuriates in her recollections of parties in the Mississippi Delta and East Tennessee. Her memory is as alive with dances, beaux, and romantic dreams as is Blanch Du Bois' in *Streetcar Named Desire* when she takes the listener on a moonlit cruise of her past, exulting over her romantic conquests and plans.[21] The disparity between Amanda's past dreams and present predicament is made all the more poignant because of the future failure to which Williams points. Even so, we pity Amanda for her striving for romance vicariously through Laura. No such romantic sentiments flicker in She's past. Hers is not the fever of excitement over dances, boys, and love. She takes an almost condescending view of her past life. The boys were ordinary, unromantically dressed, and, at worst, dull repetitions of each other. However, the romantic pulsations of young love in Williams turn into crass comments on training bras or "a chance for a feel" (p. 22) in *Counting the Ways*. Her prom evening is remembered either for its ordinariness or its mistakes. She reels even today from the scent of gardenias. Contrast this floralphobia with Amanda's craze for jonquils, a sign of her own fertility and girlish exuberance. Although She recalls the young, shy boy "during love," such memory is not a "wistfulness for real affection"[22] but a reflection of her own disinterest in conjugal lovemaking. The time past for Williams' matronly types is presented as idyllic, promising, fruitful. Memories of the past are, at best, clouded for He and She. Williams sought to capture the tender moment, however illusory or lost it is now. Albee's purpose in presenting flashbacks is to show a lack of sentimentality in love and to offer a reason, perhaps, for the lack of affection in the couple's present lives.

As a result of Albee's manipulation of the convention of the past affectionately remembered, lost affection is comic and absurd in *Counting the Ways* while it is moving and tragic in *The Glass Menagerie*. Albee's He and She simply go through the motions, or forms, of emotion, but they are, in the end, essentially devoid of feelings, perhaps because of their essential hollowness. It is hard to cry along with He over either civilization or the death of Auden because there is, in effect, no one to cry with. In contrast, Amanda's tragedy is felt because it appears to affect a real person, instead of a caricature, a character with an identity or a central core from which her own emotions are generated. Because Amanda seems real, the objects which surround her take on the air of reality. Within the play, Williams includes props which vibrate with affection—yearbooks, glass animals, dance hall lights. Such symbols enrich our appreciation of the characters' lives and reinforce Williams' desire to lay bare a tender heart. Albee's symbolism, more appropriately termed anti-symbolism, makes He and She ridiculous. The love tests, domestic symbols (chairs, tables, beds), and flowers are reduced to laughter as Albee strips away their traditional value and trust in order to reveal characters who have fled affection and warmth. Such symbols in Albee's work are purposely devoid of sentiment because of the characters' fear of intimacy. These symbols stand for the exact opposite of the values an audience would think they should have. Like many of the conventions in the play, they are familiar forms devoid of their familiar content. Albee's symbolic props lack the credulity, much less, the aura of romance.

One also sees Albee's manipulation of the more blatant "mechanics" of the romantic theatre. Williams' plastic theatre was molded by what was "dim and poetic," vague outlines alternating with bright shapes. Some of those bright shapes were to be found on the stage screens used in the first performances of *The Glass Menagerie*, the bright lights which flashed on and off with key words recording passions and failed dreams. For Williams such announcements bear the poetry of his suffering souls. In contrast, Albee's excursions into such stagecraft are bleak. His vaudevillian signs point to alienation, a tinsel advertisement characteristic of empty, unpoetic hearts. Albee's signs in the Avant Scene, identifying the title, author, and director of his play, and later telling the actors to "Identify Yourselves," were denounced as "razzmatazz illuminations from above" in the London production.[23] While there was no "flashy stage business"[24] in the Hartford production, the signs were still harsh, in some ways signifying a jarring fusion of art and reality. In any case, where the stage screens in *The Glass Menagerie* flashed sentimentally-colored cachets of romance — blue roses, the gentlemen caller — Albee's signs read like billboards at a border crossing, forbidding the audience to cross over any emotional or amorous threshold. While numerous critics have complained that such gimmickery does not work well within the play, that is exactly the point which the play was intended to make. None of these devices work because there is no larger context to give them meaning. It is the substance of Williams' play which blinds one to the artificiality of devices such as words and images flashed upon the screen. In the world of the anonymous He and She, the emptiness of both character and play demonstrate that reliance on forms devoid of substance is simply not enough for either successful living or successful art. In the case of *Counting the Ways*, that failure is deliberate and constitutes the theme which the play's critics have been so desperate to discover, so that it is the very failure of the substanceless medium which becomes the play's final message.

Notes

[1]Clive Barnes, "Stage: Double Bill by Albee," *New York Times*, 4 February 1977, p. C-4.
[2]Douglas Watt, "A Long Night of Albee," *New York Daily News*, 5 February 1977, reprinted in *Newsbank (Performing Arts)* 11 (January/February: B10.
[3]Albee directed only the Hartford production, not the London one. Albee's directorial interest in his own work may make American theatre history. Up until October 1978, he directed seven of the eight one-act plays he has written, and he frequently travels at home and abroad to see how his plays are directed. Albee's role as a director surfaces at interviews, and he has been immodestly eager to comment on his directorial talents. Stressing his dedication to "accuracy and clarity," he admits that there are dangers to authors guiding their works from the wings: "I've always assumed that when I direct my own plays I may not get the most effective productions, but I know I'll get one closest to what I intend,"

quoted in William Gover, "Albee Not on a Soap Box, But...," *Times Picayune,* 30 January 1977, Section 2, p. 11. For a discussion of Albee as director, see Malcolm Johnson, "Albee at 48: Writing, Directing, Traveling, and Thinking," *Hartford Courant,* 23 January 1977, p. 1F.

4Malcolm Johnson, "Albee Directs Albee," *Hartford Courant* (6 February 1977), p. 1F. Mark Boyer expressed equally complimentary sentiments about Albee's own translation of the play into action: "Albee directs...with a marked restraint... clarity and simplicity honor the integrity of the text" ("Premier Albee: Irresistable Rhythms, Unnatural Acts," *Hartford Advocate,* 9 February 1977, pp. 19, 26. Clive Barnes, in an otherwise mixed review, proclaimed that *Counting the Ways* was "meticulously directed by the author himself" in "Double Bill." At the same time, on either side of the Atlantic, the play was attacked for its lack of cohesiveness and sense. Irving Wardle's *London Times* review castigated *Counting the Ways* as "this sixty-minute doodle" ("Sixty-minute, second-rate doodle," *London Times,* 7 December 1976, p. 11). In a review for the *Boston Globe,* Kevin Kelly condemned *Counting the Ways* as "a pretentious, twaddling excuse for a play. It is arch, phony, sleight-of-mind intellectual" ("Albee Suffers Déjà Vu," *Boston Globe,* 10 February 1977, p. C7). William Sullivan, who had traveled to Connecticut to review the play for the *Los Angeles Times,* pronounced it a "disappointment" in part because "the larger strategy is obscure" ("A Double Bill of Pale Albee," *Los Angeles Times,* 3 February 1977, Section 4, pp. 1, 13).

5Thomas P. Adler, "*Counting the Ways* by Edward Albee," *Educational Theatre Journal* 29 (October 1977):408. Also see Gordon Rogoff, "Albee and Mamet: The War of the Words," *Saturday Review,* 2 April 1977, p. 36.

6Edward Albee, *Counting the Ways* in *Counting the Ways* and *Listening: Two Plays* (New York: Atheneum, 1977), p. 10. All subsequent page references appear in the text.

7Johnson, "Albee Directs Albee."

8Barnes, "Double Bill."

9Johnson, "Albee Directs Albee."

10Albee's playful replication begins with his dedication: "FOR BILL & WILLY / WILLY & BILL."

11Quoted in Philip Oakes, "Don't Shoot the Playwright...," *London Sunday Times,* 12 December 1976, p. 35.

12Charles C. Krohn and Julian N. Wasserman, "An Interview with Edward Albee, 3/18/81." See above, p. 19.

13"Edward Albee: An Interview," in *Edward Albee: Planned Wilderness: Interview, Essays and Bibliography,* ed. Patricia De La Fuente (Edinburg, Texas: Pan American University, 1980), pp. 16–17.

14Many critics are guilty of committing an intentional fallacy in ignoring the dramatic use to which Albee puts allusions and by focusing instead on his reading habits. Warning Albee to stop reading Henry James and T. S. Eliot, Sullivan prognosticated: "It could be terminal." More charitably, Julius Novick conceded that Albee had found a "new voice" but lamented that "it is only a whimper, or perhaps a genteel murmur," "Doing His Best," *Village Voice,* 21 February 1977, p. 99.

15Boyer, "Premier Albee."

16Quoted in Alan Wallach, "Edward Albee: 'If the Play Can Be Described in One Sentence, That Should Be Its Length,'" *Times Picayune,* 19 January 1979, Section 1, p. 4.

[17]Thomas P. Adler, "Art or Craft: Language in the Plays of Albee's Second Decade," in *Planned Wilderness*, p. 51.

[18]*The Jerome Biblical Commentary*, ed. by Raymond E. Brown, S.S.; Joseph A. Fitzmyer, S.J.; and Roland E. Murphy, O. Carm. (Englewood Cliffs, N.J.: Prentice-Hall, 1968), p. 579.

[19]Gordon Rogoff, "Albee and Mamet."

[20]This description comes from the stage direction at the beginning of Act I of the *Glass Menagerie*.

[21]Martin Gotfried, *A Theatre Divided* (Boston: Little, Brown, 1967), has said of *Streetcar:* "For it is an exquisite play—perhaps the most romantic, poetic, and sensitive play ever written for the American theatre." Much of *Streetcar*'s romance, poetry, and sensitivity were foreshadowed in the *Glass Menagerie*.

[22]Joan S. Fleckenstein, *"Counting the Ways* and *Listening* by Edward Albee," *Educational Theatre Journal* 29 (October 1977):409.

[23]Wardle, "Sixty-minute, second-rate doodle."

[24]Boyer, "Premier Albee."

The Limits of Reason
Seascape as Psychic Metaphor

LIAM O. PURDON

O NE OF THE MOST NOTABLE aspects of Edward Albee's drama has
been his recurrent interest in theatre as a means for the revelation
of psychological process, for by his own admission Albee has, as a
writer, been most interested in capturing the unconscious rhythms of
his onstage characters rather than their superficial mannerisms.
Clearly, with their extensive speeches directed to multiple audiences
and their diminished physical action, many of Albee's plays have as
their focus the motivation behind action rather than action itself. Thus
one finds that with increasing regularity Albee's work seems to include
both discussions of and metaphors for the cognitive process, so that
within his works virtually no explanation for human consciousness —
ranging from the brief discussion of the physio-electrical basis of
knowledge in *Listening* to the use of the phrenological model as a prop
in the psychological allegory, *Tiny Alice*—is left unexplored. However, it
is in *Seascape* that Albee provides one of his clearest attempts to render
his own understanding of the human psyche into extended and concrete metaphorical form. While *Tiny Alice,* dubbed by its critics as
"metafuzzical,"[1] works as an abstract treatise on human psychology,
Seascape functions in the tradition of the medieval morality play with its
more clearly defined figures serving as emblems for the distinct parts
of the human consciousness.

In rendering his own version of human psychological makeup,
Albee clearly borrows from but does not conspicuously adhere to the

141

traditional psychic zones of Freudian tripartation, for the playwright does metaphorically dramatize the tension between the forces, or principles, which pull man between his desire for reality (order) and pleasure (chaos).[2] Indeed, the principal characters, Charlie and Nancy, call the audience's attention to what might be termed the American mid-life crisis: their children grown, Charlie feels that he has earned a little rest, while Nancy believes that they have earned a little life. Yet the conflict, if it may be called that, in the central characters' purposes takes on the proportions of crisis when, at the end of the first act, Charlie and Nancy encounter Albee's dramatically unique representation of the psychic energy of the unconscious: the saurian characters, Leslie and Sarah. As symbols of such psychic energy, the primordial lizard-creatures represent both the means and the opportunity for the central characters to act upon the conflicting desires which have been kept in balance until this moment of crisis. Thus, it is through the metaphorical confrontation between the dynamic principles for reality and pleasure with the unknown saurian creatures that Albee presents his allegory of the process of the regulation of that energy, a theme which comprises the didactic matter of the play.

As the play begins, Albee first introduces the audience to this metaphor of the psyche through the characters of Charlie and Nancy. They converse as might any couple on an outing to the seashore while the intrusive sound of a jet aircraft is heard overhead. But as their dialogue continues and transforms itself into an argument, the emphasis each places on his respective point of view illustrates the tension and perennial conflict between reason and desire. Each in turn becomes a spokesman for the reality and pleasure principles. Accordingly, Nancy, who believes they have "earned a little life,"[3] argues inconsistently but passionately for the pursuit of unreproved pleasure, especially in the leisure activity of beachcombing, while Charlie, who remains circumspect and noticeably inhibited, argues for moderation and the acceptance of the *status quo*.

The revelation of the pleasure principle through the character of Nancy in Act I is developed several ways, the most noticeable of which appears in Albee's parenthetical stage directions. From the moment the curtain rises, Nancy demonstrates the full spectrum of human emotion: one moment she laughs and is gay; the next, she is sad and testy. She is enthusiastic, then taunting, and an instant later disappointed; one moment she is cheerful and matter-of-fact; the next, bitter and begrudging. Furthermore, Albee puts the intensity of Nancy's passion and her emotional capriciousness in relief by comparing it to

Charlie's stolid indifference. Even Nancy's seemingly insignificant movements on stage—her several returns to the paint box, for example —assume functional meaning, especially as they occur while Charlie remains lying in the supine position for nearly half of the first act.

In her mercurial changes of temperament and restive actions, Nancy is the embodiment of what Sigmund Freud describes as the primordial life-principle which knows "no organization and unified will, only an impulsion to obtain satisfaction."[4] Nancy is the very personification of inconsistent behavior bent on the fulfillment of appetitive desire. As such, she is the character with whom Albee associates the preparation of food. As the argument between Charlie and Nancy unfolds, it is Nancy and not Charlie who begins packing the lunch hamper. Later, as Charlie gropes for an explanation of the vision of the sea creatures and blames the whole experience on spoiled liver paste, Albee reveals that it was Nancy who had prepared the meal and chosen the fatal menu.

Yet Nancy embodies more than mere dietary appetite. In contrast to her husband, Nancy demonstrates an unrepressed appetite for the sensuous experience of nature. Arguing for a life spent by the seashore, she tells Charlie, "I love the water, and I love the air, and the sand and the dunes and the beach grass, and the sunshine on all of it and the white clouds way off, and the sunsets and the noise the shells make in the waves ... " (p. 5). Such unabashed appreciation for the sensual naturally leads to the presentation of Nancy as a creature of sexual appetite as well. Recalling the vicissitudes of their earlier married life, Nancy, not Charlie, introduces, first, the subject of infidelity and, second, the subject of coital loneliness, a modification of the concept of La Petit Morte. While she reassures Charlie by confessing that she never succumbed to her passions and desires, Nancy does, nevertheless, reveal that earlier in her marriage she was obsessed with the idea of unrestrained sexuality for a short period of time:

> Yes, but the *mind*. And what bothered me was not what you might be doing ... but that, all of a sudden, I had not. *Ever* ... All at once I thought: it was over between us ... and I thought back to before I married you, and the boys I would have done it with, if I had been that type, the firm-fleshed boys I would have taken in my arms had it occurred to me. And I began to think of them, Proust running on, pink and ribbons, looking at your back, and your back would turn and it would be Johnny Smythe or the Devlin boy, or one of the others, and he would smile, reach out a hand, undo my ribbons, draw me close, ease on. Oh, that was a troubling time (p. 22).

Yet the speech reveals more about Nancy than the nature of her sexual fantasies. While it portrays her as a creature of what Freud termed "impulsion," it shows that those natural impulses have been kept in check by external and, perhaps to Nancy, alien forces: the societal concept of "that type." Moreover, Nancy's reference to Proust is especially significant here since, within the context of the passage, it introduces the Proustian concept of absence, one of the most revealing of the 19th century literary representations of the primordial life principle of the Freudian "impulsion to obtain satisfaction." This view of love as a "subjective creation of imagination which cannot thrive in the presence of its object" explains the essential motivation behind her ephemeral infidelity.[5]

Albee completes the development of the metaphoric representation of the pleasure principle in the character of Nancy by illustrating telling idiosyncrasies of her behavior and qualifying the nature of her relationship with Charlie. Nancy, for example, is conspicuously and frequently ebullient, especially as she returns to her painting and tries to persuade Charlie "to unfetter" himself and "see everything twice" (p. 10). While originating in a natural desire, this ebullience, owing to its frequency, illustrates the frenetic condition of the "impulsion to satisfaction." Further, her thinking —often muddled and, as she herself points out, contradictory—degenerates frequently into emotionalism, which further illustrates the disorganized condition of desire. Likewise, her repeated demonstrations of peevishness—to which she, again, admits guilt as she states to Charlie almost perfunctorily, "I was being petulant" (p. 31)—reveal a disunified will. And her subordinate relationship to Charlie, which she acknowledges several times, also contributes to the metaphor of the pleasure principle in that it intimates the dynamics of mental process. This subservient status takes on significant meaning and even explains much of Nancy's argument when she begins to tell Charlie how she nearly became unfaithful and states, "The deeper your inertia went, the more *I* felt alive" (p. 21). As reason loses control of desire, the impulsion to satisfaction assumes a stronger vitality. Hence, Charlie's direct response shortly thereafter to Nancy's taunting—"You're not cruel by nature; it's not your way." (p. 17) —functions in a severalfold manner: it enables Charlie to gain the advantage in the argument, provides a statement of her character, and introduces for the audience, on the one hand, an illustration of the dynamic process by which one force keeps the other in check, and, on the other, a significant non-judgmental account of the nature of unrestrained fulfillment of satisfaction. The primordial life function is neither good nor bad; it is just the manifestation of tremendous vitality. As Freud points out: "Naturally, the id knows no values, no good and evil, no morality."[6]

As Albee uses the character of Nancy to illustrate the pleasure principle, so he likewise uses Charlie to embody the corresponding reality principle and its role of restraining, or counter-balancing, the uncontrolled impulses of the former. Thus, while Nancy refers to Proust, Charlie is through his own allusion associated with Anatole France, a figure noted for his rationalistic, dispassionate approach to art.[7] While Nancy consistently reacts through the display of emotion, Charlie reacts through reason. Thus, Charlie's first reaction to the sight of Leslie and Sarah is to posit the "logical" explanation that he and Nancy have become victims of food poisoning, a logical if incorrect means of making the unknown and irrational fit neatly into the constructs of his own world. Thus, in Charlie one finds a man who finds it easier to yield up his own life, through the assumption of his own death, than to accept that which defies his own logic and experience. While Charlie first becomes distraught at the sight of the two reptilian creatures, he quickly gains control over his emotions, in contrast to Nancy, who is immediately attracted to the creatures precisely because they seem so alien and, hence, apart from ordinary, rational experience.

However, if Charlie and Nancy are so different in their initial responses to life in general and the sea-creatures in particular, it would be a mistake to conceive of their mid-life crisis as being analogous to that of the anonymous pair in *Counting the Ways*, whose lives are shown to have grown so separate and self-contained, for the point of conflict between Nancy and Charlie is the way in which their differently directed points of view act upon each other in order to create a workable psychological balance which allows them to function successfully in the world at large. Thus, Charlie and Nancy cannot ultimately be examined in isolation since both of their identities come from the continual tug-of-war between their conflicting desires, a conflict which results in their perpetual process of dynamic self-definition and their mutual dependency rather than separateness. One sees this self-defining tug-of-war in Nancy's attempt to convince Charlie to relive his boyhood experience of submerging himself in the ocean. Charlie points out to Nancy that as a child he enjoyed sensory delight and the condition of being submerged and contained in the water:

> I used to go way down; at our summer place; a protective cove. The breakers would come in with a storm, or a high wind, but not usually. I

used to go way down, and try to stay. I remember before that, when I was tiny, I would go to the swimming pool, at the shallow end, let out my breath and sit on the bottom ... and when I was older, we were by the sea. Twelve; yes, or thirteen.
        I used to lie on the warm boulders, strip off ... learn about my body ... And I would go into the water, take two stones, as large as I could manage, swim out a bit, tread, look up one final time at the sky ... relax ... begin to go down ... just one more object come to the bottom, or living thing, part of the undulation and silence. It was very good (p. 16).

Clearly, Charlie's description of this world of "undulation and silence" is one of a state of pre-consciousness, of the mind free and unrestricted by reason and, especially, social convention which restrains impulse. Nancy's prolonged insistence that Charlie attempt to re-enact what has become just a pleasant and remote memory is her attempt to convert Charlie into her own image by returning him to a type of prelapsarian state of consciousness. Significantly, Charlie's stern resistance to this letting go of the conscious world is rooted in his self-consciousness, his awareness of himself as an adult. As in the case of Nancy's early sexual urges, it is the category, or role, imposed from without which ultimately separates Charlie from the pleasures of his youth. For both Charlie and Nancy, then, the result of this verbal give and take concerning desire and restraint is a process of self-definition through assertion and defense of their own points of view as each tries to defend his own values while converting those of the other.[8]
        Having established the tenuous balance between the two parts of the waking consciousness, Albee proceeds to examine and test that balance through the introduction of the two saurian creatures who have as their origin the hidden, subconscious world of "undulation and silence" described by Charlie much as the playwright does with Jerry's entrance into the well ordered, conventional world of Peter in *The Zoo Story* as well as in the unexpected appearance of Elizabeth in *The Lady from Dubuque*. If the appearance of the saurian creatures is intended as a litmus test of the central characters, the differences between Charlie and Nancy become apparent almost immediately. However, in order to understand these differences, it is important to recognize an important but subtle metamorphosis which occurs within the play. The first part of the play, the initial debate between Charlie and Nancy takes place in the realm of ordinary consciousness, the world of reason. It is a world in which Charlie, as a symbol of reason and convention, acts as indolent

restraint on the more active pleasure principle. The interjection of reason into that world is symbolized by the intrusive sounds of jet aircraft into the naturalistic scenery of the first act. The jets, whose sounds are heard some four times within the first act, are representatives, *par excellence,* of controlling rationality—for they are non-natural machines created through reason in order to satisfy and, hence, channel the primordial, imaginative urge to fly.

With the appearance of Leslie and Sarah that world is transformed into a realm in which the laws no longer apply and where the non-rational is in control. In this made-over world, the jet airplanes, whose presence were so strongly and frequently felt in the first act, make only one brief appearance. The terror which they inspire in Leslie and Sarah as well as the discomfort they create for Nancy show just how alien such machines are to nature. Within this context even the "reasonable" Charlie doubts their worth—"They'll crash into the dunes one day; I don't know what good they do" (p. 111)—with the result that he repeatedly emphasizes their status as mere "machines" whose imitation of the flight of birds is as unsatisfactory and incomplete as he had earlier judged a parrot's unthinking mimicry of human speech to be. Thus the formerly lethargic Charlie becomes active and aggressive and has to be restrained by the previously restive Nancy. From the first appearance of the saurian creatures, Nancy has clearly been in control. She is the first to notice their approach. As she recalls her childhood desires, she sees Leslie and Sarah emerge from the water; as she and Charlie discuss the possibility of Charlie's submerging himself, she notices that the two visitors are lying prone on the beach; and as she almost cajoles Charlie into slipping into the water, she observes that she has lost track of Leslie and Sarah. Nancy is also the first to recognize the intrinsic beauty of the visitors, although, in keeping with the function of her characterization, she does not know why she finds them aesthetically pleasing. Thus, as Charlie recoils at the sight of Leslie and Sarah and assumes a defensive posture, Nancy almost dreamily responds to Charlie's commands, extolling Leslie's and Sarah's beauty, first, with "Charlie! They're magnificent!" (p. 44) and, later, with "Charlie, I think they're absolutely beautiful. What are they?" (p. 45).

Yet if Nancy is in her element, Charlie clearly is not. From the outset, the reason and restraint which he demonstrated in the first part of the play repeatedly fail him in his dealings with the saurian intruders. His rational explanation for the appearance of the creatures as a result of "bad liver paste" is painfully inadequate, even to the non-rational, intuitive Nancy. And with the movement into the non-rational world, the playwright's function becomes the demonstration of the failure of rationality in the face of the irrational. This is, of course, a familiar theme in many of Albee's works, such as *A Delicate Balance* and *Tiny Alice*, and is no doubt responsible for Albee's interest in and adaptation of Herman Melville's "Bartleby the Scrivener."[9] Thus, as reason breaks down, Albee proceeds to give the unconscious a conscious form just as, when the restraints of marriage weakened, Nancy found herself giving form to her fantasies of premarital encounters with young men. Yet what is unique about *Seascape* is that, while Leslie's and Sarah's appearance suggests promordiality, it is not their saurian physical natures but rather the lengthy and seemingly desultory conversations which they have with Charlie and Nancy that confirm their introduction as representations of psychic energy. On the one hand, these discussions reveal an absence of the laws of logic; on the other, they demonstrate a disregard for or ignorance of social convention, moral restraint, and cognitive awareness of the totality of being — in other words, the artificial restraints imposed from without upon the "impulsion to satisfaction." In this regard, Leslie and Sarah also provide a view of the source of aggression and desire, another principal aspect of libido.[10]

As the two couples encounter each other at the beginning of Act II, they reveal fear and a lack of trust. No sooner do they introduce themselves to each other than they begin a series of dialogues which, while intended to be informative, end in futility, without the exchange of any meaningful information. Significantly, the first of these dialogues concerns eating. Interestingly, it also introduces the correlative condition of the ignorance of social convention. Charlie points out to Leslie that he does not know Leslie's eating habits. He then adds that "It'd be perfectly normal to assume you... [that is, Leslie and Sarah]... ate whatever...you ran into...you know, whatever you ran into" (p. 65). Leslie's ingenious response — "No; I don't know" (p. 65) — reveals the weakness of Charlie's assumption. But the absurdity of the assumption is not exposed until Charlie, who is striving for a simple response to Leslie's initial inquiry regarding Nancy's and his disposition, states that he and Nancy do not eat "anything that talks; you know, English" (p. 66). Nancy at this turn in the dialogue points out that parrots do talk and that people eat parrots. This revelation not only emphasizes the illogic of Charlie's second generalization, which is reinforced by Leslie who asks, "What are you saying?" (p. 66) but also brings the dialogue to an abrupt halt, as Charlie attempts a restatement of his original assumption, saying "I'm trying to tell you... we don't eat our own kind" (p. 66). Charlie does not contradict himself, but his attempt to sustain his original assumption undermines itself and meaning vanishes.

Another exchange that brings to the fore the absence of logic appears shortly afterward as Nancy shows Sarah her breasts. As in the first case, this instance also provides another view of the ignorance of social convention on the parts of the saurian creatures. The passage in question begins with the discussion of the function of clothing, another artificial convention, but soon focuses on the subject of Nancy's breasts. While Nancy conducts herself in a straightforward manner and shows no shame in the hope of enlightening Leslie and Sarah who have never seen a mammalian breast, Charlie becomes irrational at the seeming breakdown of decorum. At first Charlie demonstrates a postlapsarian prudishness when he corrects Nancy, indicating that she should say "mammary" instead of "breast" (p. 75). Next, when Sarah ingenuously beckons Leslie to see Nancy's breasts, Charlie reveals possessiveness, stating that he does not want Leslie looking at Nancy's nakedness. But when Charlie is questioned by Nancy and Leslie as to the motivation for his possessiveness and Leslie states conditionally that he does not want to see Nancy's breasts, Charlie reverses his original attitude, defending and extolling the virtue and beauty of Nancy's anatomy: "They're not embarrassing; *or* sad! They're lovely! Some women... some women... Nancy's age, they're... some women... I *love* your breasts" (p. 77). While Charlie's about-face can certainly be viewed as a positive act of acceptance, it reveals the working of the emotional rather than the cognitive consciousness because it is predicated upon pride and follows a demonstration of repressive social behavior. It is no coincidence, then, that Albee includes in his stage directions for Charlie that he is "more flustered than angry" (p. 77). What Charlie achieves is what he needs to achieve; that he finally perceives beauty through the challenging of his possessive nature, however, demonstrates the absence of logic.

While several other instances of emotionalism and non-sequiturs appear in this act, the discussion of ontology provides the best example of the suspension of the laws of reason. In an effort to explain why they are dead, the absurdity of which cannot go unnoticed, Charlie tries to explain to Leslie that created reality is an illusion and that true existence comes about through thought. Instead of being logical, Charlie becomes flustered and angry, and the dialogue degenerates into an emotional bout which concludes ironically with Charlies losing control of himself, shouting the name of Descartes:

Leslie:	Then I take it *we* don't *exist*.
Charlie:	*(Apologetic.)* Probably not; I'm sorry.
Leslie:	*(To Nancy.)* That's quite a mind he's got there.
Nancy:	*(Grudgingly defending Charlie.)* Well ... he thinks things through. (Very cheerful.) As for *me*, I couldn't care less; I'm having far too interesting a time.
Sarah:	*(Gets on all fours.)* Oh, I'm so glad!
Leslie:	*(Comes three steps down L. ridge. Puzzled.)* I *think* I exist.
Charlie:	*(Shrugs.)* Well, that's all that matters; it's the same thing....
Charlie:	What?
Leslie:	What you *said*.
Charlie:	*(Barely in control.)* DESCARTES!! DESCARTES!! I THINK: THEREFORE I AM!! *(Pause.)* COGITO ERGO SUM! I THINK: THEREFORE I AM ... (p. 108).

Leslie's comment that Charlie has "quite a mind" adds a further touch of irony, but it is Charlie's final comment concerning death as a release that confirms that logic has indeed failed. That Charlie beckons death by describing the final moments of life shows that he prefers the dissolution of life or existence and, in turn, the absence of reason. While the sound of an airplane flying overhead ends the discussion, the actual termination of the exchange of ideas, then, occurs in Charlie's demonstration of emotion. Even with the invocation of Descartes, the laws of logic remain absent.

The final fight or disagreement which draws the play to a close might also be viewed as another instance of the suspension of the laws of logic. Charlie's attempt to make Sarah cry is certainly irrational; this persistent taunting is clearly cruel. But the fight also introduces another view of the unconscious; it reveals an account of aggression. As Charlie forces Sarah to admit that she would cry her heart out if Leslie ever left her, Leslie grabs Charlie by the throat and slowly strangles him. Leslie's act of aggression is a demonstration of brute force, but as Leslie himself inplies shortly afterward in the line "Don't you talk to me about brute beast" (p. 132), Charlie's remorseless questioning illustrates a verbal manifestation of the same act. Leslie's implication also clarifies Charlie's previous statements concerning Leslie and Sarah. When Charlie begins the confrontation which nearly leads to his own strangulation, he exclaims that he does not understand his own feelings toward Leslie and Sarah: "I don't *know* what more I want. *(To Leslie and Sarah.)*

I don't know what I want for *you*. I don't know what I feel toward you; it's either love or loathing. Take your pick" (p. 128). While Charlie's ambivalence represents a lack of conscious control, the fact that he does describe his feelings toward Leslie and Sarah as being either of love or loathing represents an acknowledgement of Leslie and Sarah as being either the source of aggression or of desire.

Several other minor instances of aggression also arise in the second act, such as Charlie's continued taunting of Leslie and Sarah, but the one that brings the question of the unconscious clearly to the fore, like the fight in the conclusion, occurs when Charlie questions Sarah's fidelity. Charlie gets Sarah to admit that she has not "coupled" with anyone but Leslie; however, Leslie, who, like Nancy, is confused by the line of questioning, asks Charlie to state precisely what "are you after" (p. 128). When Charlie cannot and evades making an attempt at a conceptual understanding of his own purpose, a fight nearly breaks out—Nancy's and Sarah's joint intercession notwithstanding. The conflict which arises, then, results partly from Charlie's effrontery but mostly from a breakdown in communication. Ironically, it is Charlie, not Leslie, who is incapable of maintaining symbolic logic, although he blames Leslie for his own ineffectuality when he condescendingly adds, "Especially to someone who has no grasp of conceptual matters, who hasn't heard of half the words in the English language, who lives on the bottom of the sea and has green scales!" (p. 94).

This representation of aggression resulting from the absence of conceptual ability introduces a third way in which Albee creates the metaphor of uncontrolled psychic energy. Throughout the second act, he calls attention to the need for and the absence of a cognitive awareness of the totality of being. The latter obviously appears in all of the instances of aggression and lack of logic that appear from the moment the second act begins. The former, on the other hand, appears twice: first, early in the act, as Charlie and Leslie enter into a discussion of anatomical differences and, second, as Nancy and Charlie later attempt to explain and define the concept of emotion for Leslie and Sarah. In the discussion of the anatomical differences, Leslie and Sarah learn the distinctions between toes and fingers, arms and legs. This knowledge then leads them to an understanding of the social convention of handshaking, which they perform enthusiastically. While the information allows Leslie and Sarah to experience something they have never known, the significance of the event lies in the fact that it represents the beginning of the fusion of the conscious, embodied by Nancy and Charlie, and the unconscious self, embodied by Leslie and Sarah. In the later discussions of emotion, the same thing happens but to a greater degree. As Nancy and Charlie explain the nature of emotion to Leslie and Sarah, not only do the two couples gradually overcome the differences that separate them, but each couple also gains its own emotional equilibrium. Charlie and Nancy work out the doubts that each has felt toward the other; Leslie and Sarah learn what love is. Furthermore, through the delineation of emotion and the attainment of the awareness of social convention, Nancy and Charlie discover the means by which to keep Leslie and Sarah from retreating to the sea. Thus, as Albee indicates in the conclusion, it is through the understanding of the physical that one begins to perceive the totality of his being, but it is through the examination of the emotions, difficult as it may be, that one attains the totality of being.

Seascape, then, is much more than a fantastic dramatic experience. Like many of Albee's other plays, it is a romance. It provides a view of order in the presentation of the metaphoric representations of the reality and pleasure principles and a dissolution of that order in the symbolic representation of psychic energy. Like all romances, it possesses an essentially comic structure and so offers a resolution to the dissolution. Symbolically, that resolution appears in the form of a handshake. But as the conclusion to the second act demonstrates, the means by which order is reestablished is through the maintaining of contact with and the understanding of the subconscious: hence, the function of Nancy's unremitting insistence in the closing moments of the play that Leslie and Sarah not leave. To attain consciousness, as Albee indicates, one must be willing to enter the seascape, or Charlie's "protected cove," where land and sea—consciousness and the unconscious—meet and learn to accept the meaning of the experience. In that sense, Seascape, with its face-to-face confrontation between its creatures of the land and the sea, is not the flawed tale of unanswered evolutionary questions often described by critics[11] but is, instead, an optimistic blueprint for the development of a higher consciousness, for in Albee's mind evolution is clearly a matter of consciousness rather than form.

Notes

[1]John Chapman, "Revival of *Tiny Alice:* Still a Metafuzzical Bore," *New York Daily News (NYDN),* 30 September 1969, contained in *New York Theatre Critic Reviews (NYTCR),* 1969, p. 256.

[2]For a brief discussion of these two principles, see Sigmund Freud, *A General Introduction to Psychoanalysis,* trans. by Joan Riveire (New York: Garden City, 1943), pp. 311–2.

[3]Edward Albee, *Seascape* (New York: Atheneum, 1975), p. 37. All future page references appear in the text.

[4]Sigmund Freud, *New Introductory Lectures on Psychoanalysis,* trans. by W. J. H. Sprott (New York: Norton, 1933), pp. 102ff.

[5]Geoffrey Brereton, *A Short History of French Literature* (Middlesex, England: Penguin, 1968), p. 243.

[6]Freud (Sprott), p. 105.

[7]Brereton, p. 232.

[8]In this, Charlie and Nancy are much like George and Martha of *Who's Afraid of Virginia Woolf?* Like Charlie and Leslie, George and Martha seem to embody dispassionate intellect and unrestrained sexuality locked in perpetual, self-defining battle. As becomes apparent at the end of the play, their verbal battles are not symptoms of the breaking apart of their marriage but, rather, the dynamic force which binds the two differently directed individuals together: hence, Martha's vigorous defense of George at the play's end. For a discussion of similarities between *Virginia Woolf* and *Seascape,* see Howard Kissel, "Seascape," *Women's Wear Daily,* 27 January 1975, reprinted in *NYTCR,* 1975, p. 370.

[9]Albee completed an unpublished libretto adaptation of Melville's short story in 1961.

[10]Freud (Sprott), pp. 140ff.

[11]See Edwin Wilson, "Disturbing Creatures of the Deep," *Wall Street Journal,* 28 January 1975, reprinted in *NYTCR,* 1975, p. 370. For the view that the play ends optimistically, see Henry Hewes, "Theatre," *Saturday Review,* 8 March 1975, p. 40, as well as Sam Coale, "The Visions of Edward Albee," *Providence Journal,* 28 December 1975. Reprinted in *Newsbank (Literature)* (Nov.-Dec., 1975), p. A3, and Clive Barnes, "Albee's *Seascape* is a Major Event," *New York Times,* 27 January 1975 reprinted in *NYTCR,* 1975, p. 368.

Index